Dr. Jim Decker provides insightful lessons from his failures and successes. He takes us on a personal journey, intertwining leadership principles with fast-paced changes in healthcare. His experiences highlight that leadership is not a checklist but an art form.

—Dr. Kevin J. Belanger DHA, MA, MS, MT(ASCP), SBB

Reviving the Heart of Leadership enlightens the reader on how the dynamics of healthcare require agility, focus, and balance. Dr. Decker's forty-plus years of leadership experiences provide important insights into the complex world of healthcare and should be required reading for healthcare managers at every level.

—Joseph D. McDonald, FACHE
President Emeritus, Catholic Health System of Western New York

I've had the honor of working for Jim Decker in two of the hospitals mentioned in this book. First, as an "orderly" while attending college in Knoxville, then several years later as a member of his senior leadership team in Clarksville. Throughout his career, it has been evident that Jim Decker always remained grounded in his faith and excelled due to his commitment to service and desire to be a lifelong learner. This book provides a wonderful overview of a well-respected healthcare leader's career and highlights many lessons learned that will benefit all who read it.

—Gordon B. Ferguson, FACHE
President and CEO, Ascension Saint Thomas Rutherford Hospital

Jim Decker is a seasoned executive leader who leveraged his skills as a hospital executive into success in a very dynamic and challenging time in the blood/transfusion industry. As CEO, Jim faced challenges such as COVID-19 head-on, and because of his leadership, he positioned his organization as a leading regional blood center in Eastern Tennessee. *Reviving the Heart of Leadership* shares many of his professional experiences and helps to reinforce the importance of strong and compassionate leadership.

—Bill Block
CEO, Blood Centers of America, Inc.

Healthcare leadership is more than strategy—it's about resilience, adaptability, and compassion. In *Reviving the Heart of Leadership*, Dr. Jim Decker draws on four decades of experience to reveal how adversity—from policy shifts to the COVID-19 crisis—can transform leaders. Through powerful, real-world insights, he challenges executives to move beyond management frameworks and embrace leadership rooted in empathy, integrity, and purpose. This compelling guide is a must-read for healthcare professionals seeking to lead with strength, heart, and lasting impact.

—Dr. Zoher Kapasi, PT, PhD, MBA
Dean, College of Health Professions, Medical University of South Carolina

Reviving the Heart of Leadership provides an indispensable toolkit for healthcare executives who aspire to lead with compassion while navigating the complexities of today's healthcare landscape. With nearly five decades of experience, Dr. Decker provides invaluable lessons on leading transformation and addressing the unique challenges of healthcare leadership with empathy and insight. By leveraging his extensive experience managing through the historical changes in payment, policy, and healthcare delivery, Dr. Decker illustrates how current and future generations of healthcare leaders can lead effectively and compassionately. This book is an essential resource for any leader dedicated to making a meaningful impact in healthcare.

—Dr. Jillian Harvey, PhD, MPH
Director, Doctor of Healthcare Administration Division,
Medical University of South Carolina

I witnessed first-hand the challenges Jim Decker faced during his years as a hospital CEO in Tennessee. The stories he shares speak to his perseverance as well as his commitment to service and compassionate leadership. *Reviving the Heart of Leadership* should be on the mandatory reading list for all aspiring healthcare executives.

—Craig Becker, FACHE
Former President and CEO, Tennessee Hospital Association

Jim Decker was leading with heart, compassion, and genuineness long before those qualities were admired in leadership. This insightful book details his journey through many trials, revealing how not just to survive, but thrive. It's packed with practical wisdom for every leader—healthcare leaders, civic leaders, faith leaders—all who feel called to lead from the heart.

—Dr. Brent P. McDougal
Senior Pastor, First Baptist Church, Knoxville, Tennessee

REVIVING

THE

HEART

OF

LEADERSHIP

JAMES L. DECKER
DHA, LFACHE

REVIVING
THE
HEART
OF
LEADERSHIP

EMPOWERING HEALTHCARE EXECUTIVES
TO LEAD WITH COMPASSION

Advantage | Books

Published by Advantage Books, Charleston, South Carolina.
An imprint of Advantage Media.

ADVANTAGE is a registered trademark, and the Advantage colophon is a trademark of Advantage Media Group, Inc.

Printed in the United States of America.

10 9 8 7 6 5 4 3 2 1

ISBN: 978-1-64225-840-0 (Paperback)
ISBN: 978-1-64225-839-4 (eBook)

Library of Congress Control Number: 2025902364

Cover design by Lance Buckley.
Layout design by Megan Elger.

This publication is designed to provide accurate and authoritative information in regard to the subject matter covered. It is sold with the understanding that the publisher is not engaged in rendering legal, accounting, or other professional services. If legal advice or other expert assistance is required, the services of a competent professional person should be sought.

Advantage Books is an imprint of Advantage Media Group. Advantage Media helps busy entrepreneurs, CEOs, and leaders write and publish a book to grow their business and become the authority in their field. Advantage authors comprise an exclusive community of industry professionals, idea-makers, and thought leaders. For more information go to **advantagemedia.com**.

03-19-2025 2:50

*This book is dedicated to the hundreds of thousands of
healthcare professionals across our great country.
Their dedication, service, and compassion
epitomize the heart of leadership.*

CONTENTS

PART TWO

PART THREE

ACKNOWLEDGMENTS

This book was written from the heart, not by an expert. I am a regular guy who was fortunate to work in healthcare for over forty-seven years. I hope readers find my stories and experiences interesting and helpful as we navigate common challenges together.

As in healthcare, writing a book requires a team effort. I thank the Advantage | Forbes Books team for their guidance and advice. I could not have made this journey without them at my side. The input of Caroline Moore, Lauren Steffes, and especially Bud Ramey has been invaluable.

I thank my former mentors, coworkers, and professional colleagues for their support throughout my career. In particular, I wish to acknowledge the following individuals who willingly shared their insight and experiences (listed alphabetically): Craig Becker, Jack Bryan, Gordon Ferguson, Jim Goodloe, Bob Humphrey, Bart Hove, Rudy McKinley, Jim Montgomery, David Parmer, Bill Walter, Alan Watson, and Jim Whitlock.

I express appreciation for my parents (now deceased), who always encouraged me to do my best. I credit them for being the model of compassion and heart for service.

Thanks especially to my wife, Michelle, for believing in me and being patient as I sacrificed other important responsibilities to write this book. She was at my side the entire way. To my children and their spouses—Ben, Brittany (Brian), and Madeline (Zach)—and my three grandchildren (Jonah, Nolan, and Will), whose youth and enthusiasm serve as my daily inspiration.

And finally, to my high school English teacher, Ms. Bernice Rives, who must be smiling from above with the thought that I successfully authored a complete manuscript using correct grammar, spelling, and punctuation.

ADAPTIVE CAPACITY

While drafting this manuscript, I struggled with its primary purpose, focus, and intended audience. In broad terms, I describe the myriad leadership challenges that healthcare executives might encounter during their professional careers. Using my experiences as examples, I aimed to highlight the good and the bad, the highs and the lows, the successes and failures. I also interjected the perspectives of some of my professional colleagues to illustrate common challenges and experiences further.

As the book took shape, a recurring theme emerged that speaks to the essence of leadership, be it in healthcare or any other field: extraordinary leaders persevere, even in the face of adversity.

Leadership is rarely well scripted. Despite our best efforts through education and professional experience, unforeseen challenges inevitably arise. Some can be managed in due course, but others call for immediate action and a change in direction. The dynamic, ever-changing nature of healthcare means that dealing with the unexpected has become the norm, not the exception. In these moments of crisis, the resilience and adaptability of healthcare leaders truly shine, earning them our admiration and respect.

A few years ago, I read an article that resonated profoundly. While not explicitly directed at healthcare leaders, its core message echoed in my mind. The article "Crucibles of Leadership" by Warren Bennis and Robert Thomas, published in the *Harvard Business Review* in 2002, posits that great leaders possess the resolve and ability to confront adversity.[1]

The authors use the term "crucible" to describe significant events and experiences that can fundamentally transform leadership skills. They define a crucible as a transformative experience through which an individual comes to a new or altered sense of identity. Whether anticipated or not, these experiences can be navigated successfully, resulting in confident leaders with enhanced adaptive capacity to face adversity.

Healthcare can be a landmine field of crucibles in many shapes and sizes. Some emerge because of legislative or regulatory mandates. Others result from environmental changes, such as competitive pressures or volatile economic conditions. The COVID-19 pandemic is an excellent example of a crucible that posed unprecedented worldwide adversity.

Sometimes, crucibles may be in the form of personal traumatic events such as serious illness, injury, or the death of a loved one. How leaders adapt to such events can enhance their overall leadership proficiency. This underscores the importance of adaptive capacity in healthcare leadership, instilling a sense of urgency among executives to develop and strengthen this skill.

Throughout this book, I highlight examples of crucibles to emphasize events or developments requiring adaptive capacity. As relates to my professional career, most of these have been legislative

---

[1] Warren Bennis and Robert Thomas, "Crucibles of Leadership," *Harvard Business Review*, September 2002, https://hbr.org/2002/09/crucibles-of-leadership.

or regulatory mandates that affected US healthcare or community-specific issues that emerged. Then, on a more personal level, a few "life happens" events altered my outlook on life and significantly influenced my approach to leadership. Here are my crucibles that I will describe to you in the coming pages. An excellent exercise would be to list your own crucibles as you go on this journey with me.

CRUCIBLES

Crucible #1: Medicare Prospective Payment System

Crucible #2: Managed Care

Crucible #3: Clinton Healthcare Plan of 1993

Crucible #4: TennCare

Crucible #5: Balanced Budget Act of 1997

Crucible #6A: The Leapfrog Group

Crucible #6B: JCAHO National Patient Safety Goals Program

Crucible #7: Head-On Collision

Crucible #8: Patient Blood Management and the 2008 Recession

Crucible #9: Robbed at Gunpoint

Crucible #10: COVID-19

As we recount the good and the bad, the highs and the lows, the successes and the failures, I hope the key ingredients of care and compassion are always preserved. An important lesson I have learned is that navigating adversity often requires an intentional reviving of the heart of leadership.

PART ONE

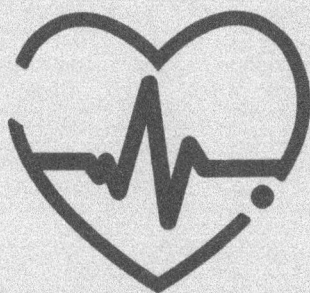

NO RESPECT

There was a time when the US healthcare system wasn't respected from a business standpoint. Then, a sea of change occurred. Healthcare embraced electronic medical records, we engaged consultants to help us navigate governmental oversight and reimbursement, and insurance companies began to demand lower costs. We had to sharpen our pencils and become accountable for a reimbursement system chided for twenty-five-dollar aspirin. In the face of a disgusted corporate world weary of high, often unexplainable hospital bills, we had a choice: embrace cost containment, improve quality, or go under.

Our ability to manage costs and turn these significant community assets into an accountable business morphed rapidly throughout my forty-seven-year career. Scientific advancements occurred daily, and fantastic change was all around us. While that advanced business acumen is still ever advancing, we got the attention of the nation and the world when we became the front line for a deadly plague, a pandemic that struck fear into everyone. We stood strong. Our nurses, doctors, and hospital team faced life-threatening danger every day, and we again won the love, admiration, and respect of every American. But there was a cost. Many hospitals found themselves in financial turmoil.

The business world can learn much from the journey of healthcare executives in the last few decades—resilience, commitment, leadership, and calmness under pressure, to name a few.

US COVID-19 DEATHS[2]
AS OF MAY 2022

16% OF ALL COVID-19 DEATHS WERE AMERICANS

BY MAY 2022, ABOUT **1 IN EVERY 328 AMERICANS** HAD DIED

CALIFORNIA HAD THE HIGHEST DEATH TOLL, WITH MORE THAN **90,000 DEAD**

TEXAS **86,000 DEAD**

FLORIDA **76,000 DEAD**

APPROXIMATELY **9 MILLION PEOPLE WERE GRIEVING** A FAMILY MEMBER KILLED BY COVID-19

---

2   Arielle Mitropoulos, "'Unthinkable Tragedy': US COVID-19 Death Toll Surpasses 1 Million," ABC News, May 12, 2022, https://www.goodmorningamerica.com/news/story/unthinkable-tragedy-us-covid-19-death-toll-surpasses-84502918.

I have managed and guided healthcare organizations for over four decades and have a profound passion for America's healthcare system. But I have retired at a time when I fear for the future. I see a continually growing cloud of turmoil and uncertainty, perhaps now more than ever.

The COVID-19 pandemic exposed major US healthcare flaws, some of which flew under the radar prepandemic. The challenges brought about by this three-year crisis accelerated their exposure further. Staffing shortages, supply chain disruptions, and increased financial pressures prompted new challenges to maintaining quality healthcare delivery.

Since 2020, when the World Health Organization declared COVID-19 a worldwide pandemic, our healthcare delivery system has seen widespread hospital closures, localized discontinuation of critical services, and publicly expressed concerns over the quality of care. These developments have significant economic and trust ramifications for main-street America, tragically affecting access to needed healthcare services in many communities nationwide.

More fallout involves the loss of long-term and seasoned leaders in the industry.

Wait, I just called healthcare an industry. We unconsciously do that. Why? Because we have been too focused on the scaffolding of leadership instead of embracing the heart of leadership.

I have had difficulty deflecting my impulse to call us the "healthcare industry." We have been doing that to ourselves for years.

The word "industry" has been removed from this manuscript when applied to describe what the men and women of US healthcare are all about. The pandemic provided the definition. These people ran directly into the disaster, not from it. Industry is "economic activity concerned with the processing of raw materials and manufacture of goods in factories."[3]

Planned and unplanned retirements, forced terminations, and just plain burnout affect our nursing and clinical teams and precipitate a mass exodus of healthcare CEOs and key management staff.[4] According to a study conducted by the *Washington Post* in collaboration with the Kaiser Family Foundation, almost 30 percent of doctors, nurses, and other caregivers have chosen to leave the profession, throwing their hands up at the mounting stress and pressures.[5]

Some portray the healthcare field as being in a state of crisis. I certainly do. But with crisis also comes opportunity. As legend has it, Winston Churchill often mused:

Never let a good crisis go to waste.[6]

Indeed, a crisis may be used as a catalyst for innovation, transformation, and change. The business world has much to learn from the journey of healthcare executives in the last few decades: resilience, commitment, leadership, and calmness under pressure, to name a few.

My career includes various administrative positions at five healthcare organizations, mainly as a hospital CEO and, more recently, as a

---

3   "Industry," Glossary, Wilson Center, https://www.wilsoncenter.org/glossary-0.

4   "Covid Burnout Hitting All Levels of the Workforce," *The Harvard Gazette*, March 31, 2023, https://news.harvard.edu/gazette/story/2023/03/covid-burnout-hitting-all-levels-of-health-care-workforce/.

5   Mark Hagland, "Washington Post/KFF Survey," Healthcare Innovation, April 23, 2021, https://www.hcinnovationgroup.com/policy-value-based-care/staffing-professional-development/news/21219802/washington-post-kff-survey-fully-29-percent-of-healthcare-workers-might-leave-the-field.

6   "Never Let a Good Crisis Go to Waste," PubMed, accessed February 28, 2024, https://pubmed.ncbi.nlm.nih.gov/36433903/.

community blood center CEO. Change never slows in healthcare. I witnessed the spirit and dedication of those who have chosen healthcare as a profession. I can't adequately express my admiration and respect for the people who devote their lives to the service of others, a noble and compassionate calling.

AN EARLY EYE-OPENING EXPERIENCE

I experienced this firsthand well before deciding to pursue a career in healthcare administration. As a college student in the early 1970s, still searching for professional direction, I worked part time as a respiratory therapist at a local hospital. At the time, I was thinking about becoming a physician and thought this real-life experience would help me achieve that goal. The extra spending money I earned was a bonus.

Working the graveyard shift from 11:00 p.m. to 7:00 a.m. allowed me to attend classes during the day. An afternoon nap reenergized me enough to do it again the next night. That experience changed my career goals and led me in a different professional direction.

I admired my fellow workers, especially those who chose to work the night shift. I learned that it takes a multidisciplinary team of professionals to deliver quality patient care, from physicians, nurses, and therapists to dieticians, cooks, and custodians. All had important jobs to do, and their dedication impressed me.

That early experience also opened my eyes to the multiple moving pieces that went into managing a hospital. I began asking questions of my coworkers and supervisors to learn what makes a hospital tick. My initial motive for working as a respiratory therapist was to gain direct patient care experience and enhance my clinical knowledge. Still, I questioned whether I might be better suited for a different role.

Healthcare was much more complex than I had thought. It was more than just doctors, nurses, and respiratory therapists. I realized that healthcare requires a team effort. How all those moving pieces were coordinated became the focus of my interest and attention. Who is in charge? Who makes the decisions regarding staffing, equipment, facilities, and supplies? Someone has to be in a position of authority to ensure that all the pieces fit.

A close boyhood friend had grown up walking the halls of a hospital. His father was the administrator of my hometown hospital. Because of our close friendship, I felt comfortable contacting my friend's father for his perspective. I made an appointment to meet with him to get his insight and advice. After a brief but productive meeting, he gave me some material to read and encouraged me to consider a career in hospital administration. To this day, I credit him with planting that seed in my mind.

A LASTING IMPRESSION

I recall one specific event that made a lasting impression on me and, more than any other experience, influenced my future career decision.

One night, I was working my regular shift when I received a physician's order to hook up an oxygen cannula on a young teenage boy. Since most of my patients were elderly, suffering from chronic respiratory problems, I was taken aback when asked to administer oxygen to a teenager.

Per protocol, I checked with the charge nurse before entering the patient's room. The nurse cautioned me to use extra special precautions before entering the patient's room and that wearing a gown, mask, and gloves would be a good idea. That is when it became apparent to me that I was dealing with a patient with a severe diagnosis. This young teenager was battling spinal meningitis.

I vividly recall seeing the patient's mother anxiously pacing the floor. I entered the room, introduced myself to the mother, hooked up the oxygen humidifier, and placed the cannula around the patient's head. There was no movement, reaction, or response whatsoever from the patient. I quietly exited the room, disposed of the protective clothing, and returned to the nurses' station.

Over the next several hours, as I made my rounds and conducted my routine assignments, I couldn't help but think of that young teenager. Periodically, I would visit the nurses' station to check on his status. On a typical night, I would start preparing my report for the day-shift staff around 6:30 or 6:45 a.m., but that night was different.

Around 4:30 a.m., I noticed activity outside that patient's room. Alarms sounded, and conversations between coworkers were noticeably more direct and tense; I heard no laughter or casual conversation. The sounds of rolling crash carts, fast-paced footsteps, and the clanging of various pieces of equipment filled the air.

A constant stream of people flowed in and out of the patient's room for several minutes: physicians, nurses, technicians, therapists, and nursing aides. I entered and held an oxygen mask on the patient's face while an experienced team of professionals did their best to revive this young patient.

I remember how nervous I was, knowing I had a critical job. Even with my knees shaking uncontrollably, I knew I had to remain focused. Sadly, after what seemed to be several hours, and despite the valiant efforts of those dedicated caregivers, this young boy was pronounced dead.

I watched as the mother grieved. Tears were flowing down her cheeks. I heard her shouts of anguish, her pleas of "Why?" and her vocal expressions of love for her child. I also found it difficult to control my own emotions.

The best I could do was to follow the prescribed protocol, take inventory of the equipment and supplies, dispose of my protective gear, and make the appropriate notations in the patient's chart. I did so with an external calmness that was expected of me, but inside, I was an emotional wreck.

I gathered myself, then walked the long corridor back to our department, where I sat, staring at the wall for several hours. I know I provided a report to the day-shift staff, but I have little recollection. I never made it to my classes that day.

Almost fifty years later, I reflect on those long nights and see healthcare through different eyes. Those early experiences gave me unique insight that has remained with me throughout my career. I spent most of my career in the C-suite, entrusted with leading and making important decisions for my respective organizations. However, I saw things differently with each decision, especially those affecting staff and patients. I witnessed the importance of compassionate care from the perspective of the frontline staff, and equally as important, I was able to see things from the perspective of a patient and a patient's family.

ACADEMIC PREPARATION

I entered graduate school at the University of Alabama at Birmingham (UAB) in the fall of 1975, having been accepted into the master's degree program in hospital and health administration. I moved to a new school, city, and state, so it was a new adventure. I had spent the previous six years at Louisiana State University (LSU) studying microbiology. Other than a few courses in accounting and economics,

I hadn't been exposed to anything resembling management or administration. It was all very new to me.

Back then, at least in my small-town high school, there wasn't much career guidance for graduating seniors. Excellent female students were encouraged to enter nursing or education, while excellent male students were encouraged to pursue medicine or law. I chose medicine, never really giving it much serious thought.

Once I got to college, I primarily took premed courses: chemistry, biology, physics, etc. Outside of the required courses within the premed curriculum, the electives I took mainly were fun courses like speech, tennis, and art appreciation. One exception is that I took calculus as an elective because I thought it would look good on my transcript.

Leadership is not easy. The perception that executives have it easy in their plush corner offices, aided by layers of administrative assistants, is misguided. Granted, leaders are often placed in the spotlight and receive public accolades, which tend to paint a rosy picture when things are going well. Yet the perceived fame and fortune can also mask the agony of gut-wrenching decisions, strained relationships, and countless sleepless nights that come with the job. Influential leaders work hard to keep it all in balance.

I hope my story becomes more than just another book on leadership. I intend to speak to the heart and soul of healthcare workers, sharing real-life experiences, stories, and broad-based perspectives about leadership. My stories and the stories of my professional colleagues will serve as examples to illustrate the importance of solid but compassionate leadership.

Much has been written about servant leadership and how those who embody that leadership style make a lasting and meaningful impression. Based on the seminal work of Robert K. Greenleaf, a former AT&T executive who coined the term almost thirty years ago, servant leadership emphasizes an emerging approach to leadership—one that prioritizes serving others, including employees, customers, and the community.

Consider this book as an effort to effectively blend the tenets of servant leadership with the unique challenges of healthcare leadership.[7] If the healthcare system we rely upon has entered a state of crisis, then this is a perfect time to influence the future. I believe that healthcare is poised to leverage this crisis for the better. We would be guilty of a missed opportunity if we "let a good crisis go to waste."

But it goes beyond academic preparation. In the US, we are fortunate to have an impressive list of graduate programs that address the educational side of the equation. We have outstanding professional organizations, such as the American College of Healthcare Executives (ACHE), that provide professional credentialing and continuing education for healthcare leaders. Leadership, however, involves so much more in terms of passion, calling, compassion, and empathy.

I want to help prepare the next generation of healthcare workers. I want to help them understand the unique challenges faced by those in leadership positions and provide some insight into the decision-making process. I recognize that healthcare executives are sometimes painted as stiff, hard to read, and financially motivated. This characterization may be true in some cases.

However, I have also seen examples throughout my career where successful leaders, when faced with difficult decisions, often consider other important factors, not just the potential impact on the bottom line. I want to ensure that these leadership qualities and those who exhibit them get appropriate recognition and respect. My nonhealthcare friends say that the pressures I have experienced are significantly

---

7   Robert K. Greenleaf, *The Power of Servant-Leadership* (Berrett-Koehler Publishers, 1998).

more intense than those in the typical corporate world. Considering the notion "That which does not kill me only makes me stronger," I tell the story of my journey.

CHAPTER 1

THE CURVEBALL

> *Like any other job interview, I was asked about my educational background, work history, and career goals. I knew those questions were coming, so I was ready. I was confident and prepared. I had done my homework. Then came the curveball:*
>
> *"Mr. Decker, how would you describe your leadership style?"*

The healthcare field has endured significant change in recent years. One could argue, however, that more change is needed. Other sectors of our society are also experiencing changes, some even more radical than those we have seen in healthcare. Technology and the financial markets are two notable examples.

As is true with many aspects of life, change gives rise to new challenges and opportunities. While healthcare may not necessarily be unique, what makes it different?

The answer is rather obvious from my perspective. From large institutions such as hospitals and health systems to individual practitioners such as physicians and nurses, healthcare involves life-and-death issues. The health and well-being of people are at stake. Health-care touches the mind, body, and soul like no other industry.

While some consider the Affordable Care Act (a.k.a. "Obamacare") the most transformational healthcare legislation of our lifetime, it still hasn't fixed all the problems. Granted, it has elevated the focus on the quality of care and improved access to healthcare services through broadened insurance options. But the financial pressures still exist.

Healthcare leaders are in a difficult position. We must balance compassion for others with financial realities. We must empathize with our key stakeholders (patients, families, employees) and be attuned to their individual and collective needs. However, we also have a fiduciary responsibility to balance the budget and lead our respective organizations in a financially prudent manner. We often find ourselves caught between the proverbial rock and a hard place.

The leadership qualities necessary to navigate through these complex issues are essential. I worked in various leadership positions in healthcare for forty-seven years. Early in my career, the importance of those leadership qualities wasn't always on my radar. I was more focused on my own personal goals and career advancement. But, with time, experience, and the wisdom I gained from others, I eventually learned some crucial lessons.

A PIVOTAL INTERVIEW

A defining moment for me came sometime in the mid-1990s. At the time, I had almost twenty years of professional experience and had an established track record. I had progressed through several midlevel administrative positions and tasted success as CEO at two different hospitals. Then, one day, the call came as I sat at my desk. It was from an executive recruiter who wanted to assess my interest in a CEO position at an extensive, prestigious health system. His call got my attention.

Anyone who has gone through this process knows the drill. I quickly updated my résumé, highlighted a few more professional accomplishments, and mailed him a copy with a carefully worded cover letter. Then came the waiting game. The recruiter needed time to receive my information, review my credentials, and determine if my background and experience were worthy of consideration. If so, I would be invited for an interview.

A few weeks later, his follow-up call came, and an interview was scheduled. I cleared my calendar and made the necessary travel arrangements. The interview was held in the recruitment firm's office in downtown Atlanta.

As any interested candidate would do, I also conducted my due diligence by learning as much as possible about the health system. The search firm mailed me a packet of printed material, unlike today when a wealth of information is readily available on the internet. I also conducted a private rehearsal session to be mentally prepared for the questions posed during the interview.

And, of course, I carefully selected the right business suit, shirt, and tie for the occasion. I got a fresh haircut, I ensured my clothes were cleaned and pressed, and my shoes had that extra-special shine. I had all the bases covered.

ICE WATER FLOWING THROUGH MY VEINS

Like many other endeavors (sports, music, etc.), preparation was complex, but I was prepared and ready for the main event. I was confident, calm, and collected. The first few minutes of the interview went as expected. I sensed that things were going well, and from my perspective, all was going as planned.

> *Like any other job interview, I was asked about my educational background, work history, and career goals. I knew those questions were coming, so I was ready. I was confident and prepared. I had done my homework. Then came the curveball. "Mr. Decker, how would you describe your leadership style?"*

At that moment, my chin was the only thing breaking in a downward motion. I was not ready for this. For some reason, I felt that my personal space had been invaded. Why would anyone be interested in my leadership style? My educational background, professional experience, and track record should speak for themselves. When the question came, so did a sense of uneasiness.

I paused for a moment, gathered my thoughts, and tried to formulate an intelligent response. My eyes gazed at the ceiling, my stomach tightened, and beads of sweat formed on my forehead.

Then, with the confidence I had demonstrated in my previous responses, I boldly said, "I have a participative leadership style. I focus on assembling a strong and talented team; then, I rely on the team's expertise and what they contribute. My job is to create, cultivate, and encourage a collaborative spirit to serve the organization's best interests."

The recruiter nodded politely, which signaled that my response was well received. But obviously, I didn't provide enough detail to satisfy the recruiter. When asked to elaborate further (the always dreaded follow-up question), I uncharacteristically started to ramble, and my nervousness began to show.

"I don't particularly care for the autocratic or authoritative management style. I don't enjoy barking out orders and telling people what to do. I don't consider myself a 'bossy boss.' I enjoy coaching, advising, and mentoring. The participative leadership style seems to fit my personality best."

I didn't get the job, but it wasn't because of my response to that one question. The individual they hired was better qualified. Nevertheless, I will never forget that interview. It made me much more conscious of how different leadership styles affect an organization. I have read numerous books on leadership and have attended countless leadership conferences and seminars. I have even taught a course on healthcare leadership at a local college. I certainly don't profess to be an expert, but I am more aware of different leadership styles than ever before.

WHAT WOULD RAY BROWN DO?

Leadership styles can vary from person to person. No two people are exactly alike, and no two people deal with issues similarly. Like one's personality, a leader's style is unique to that individual. More importantly, the values, character, and judgment of people in leadership positions often serve as the true compass for establishing organizational direction.

In my second quarter at UAB, I took an elective course on current issues in healthcare. The course was taught by the CEO of the university hospital in Birmingham, and the class was held in his office at 8:00 a.m. on Tuesdays. There were only eight students in the course, and we were greeted each morning by the CEO's administrative assistant, who offered us a cup of freshly brewed coffee and an assortment of freshly baked pastries. Once class started, we spent the first few minutes shooting the bull and talking about sports, then watched the CEO put on his necktie, comb his hair, and arrange papers on his desk.

Frequently, as would be expected, we weren't the only ones in the executive suite at that time of the morning. There was a steady stream of people—department managers, physicians, board members—in and out of the administrative offices. It was like Grand Central Station.

There were days when the start time of the class had to be delayed while the CEO dealt with more pressing matters. I remember one morning when an angry doctor showed up, unannounced, demanding to meet with the CEO. This obviously took precedence over our class time. For twenty to thirty minutes, the CEO and doctor huddled in a private conference room, only to reappear with smiles and handshakes. The CEO then turned his attention to us, and we proceeded with class as if nothing had happened.

The course was a seminar course, meaning that we would come prepared to discuss current healthcare developments. We were assigned weekly readings on various topics, and one student was assigned to provide a detailed summary of an emerging healthcare issue. The capstone assignment for the course was to read a book on healthcare leadership, write a paper summarizing the book's key points, and deliver a verbal presentation to the class.

The book I chose for this assignment was *Judgment in Administration* by Ray E. Brown. This book was written in 1966, and its author was a well-respected hospital executive. Ray Brown is considered one of the true pioneers of hospital administration.

As I recall, I randomly chose this book from a list of suggested titles, not knowing anything about the author or what the book was about. However, I have reflected on this book numerous times during my professional career. Etched in my mind is the true meaning of the word "judgment" and its importance as it relates to how leaders conduct themselves.[8] I wish I could say I always exercised good

---

8   Ray E. Brown, *Judgment in Administration* (McGraw-Hill, 1966).

judgment in my actions and decisions, but I can't. Yet many times over the years when faced with a difficult decision, I have asked myself, "What would Ray Brown do?"

JUDGMENT

Fast-forward about forty-five years: as part of my doctoral studies at the Medical University of South Carolina, I read another book on the same topic as the one I read during my graduate studies. This book, *Judgment* by Noel Tichy and Warren Bennis, took a deeper dive into the importance of exercising sound judgment in decision-making.[9] In a somewhat ironic but poignant way, I read these two books at two entirely different stages of my professional career. Perhaps they were meant to serve as "bookends" to emphasize the importance of that critical leadership quality.

I have been fortunate to be associated with many talented and successful healthcare executives. Some I had the opportunity to work with or for, and others I only knew professionally or observed from a distance. One constant trait that all possessed was impeccable judgment when confronted with critical decisions or situations. As I think about it, this should come as no big surprise. The most crucial trait boards of directors look for in selecting CEOs is their decision-making ability, which includes exercising good judgment.

TWENTY-TWENTY HINDSIGHT

Webster defines "judgment" as "pronouncing a formal opinion or decision."[10] This may sound legalistic and narrow in focus, yet during

---

9   Noel M. Tichy and Warren G. Bennis, *Judgment* (Portfolio, 2007).

10   "Judgment," *Merriam-Webster*, accessed February 2024, https://www.merriam-webster.com/dictionary/judgement.

any given day, healthcare leaders are faced with hundreds of decisions. Granted, some of them are not mission critical, but they may still have an important bearing on the organization. Others may be critical and may have immediate and long-lasting consequences. The term "judgment" also implies that the individual doing the judging can distinguish between right and wrong. In my opinion, therein lies the most fundamental aspect of exercising good judgment.

Exercising good judgment in administration is a trait that all good leaders should possess. But is that always the case? I fear that some of the problems the US healthcare system is experiencing today result from poor judgment by key decision-makers.

To be fully transparent, I would include myself in that number. I will admit that clouded judgment led me to make some ill-advised decisions during my career. Twenty-twenty hindsight would suggest that I should have handled certain situations differently. Hopefully, I learned from those experiences.

It is time for those of us in leadership positions to change course before we reach the point of no return. A different focus might be the best remedy for what ails us. Could a healthy dose of compassion, servant leadership, and better judgment be just what the doctor has ordered?

ARE LEADERS BORN OR MADE?

There are many published articles and books on leadership. Some address the question "Are leaders born or made?"

My answer is "yes."

Allow me to use myself as an example. My leadership style blends the personality traits of my father with the practical leadership approach I learned by observing Tom Newland, my first early-career mentor.

My dad was a man of few words. He was quiet and reserved—never the life of the party. He did more listening than talking, but when he spoke, others listened. He was raised to treat other people the way he wanted to be treated. Yet, in his mild-mannered way, he garnered tremendous respect from others.

As I have grown older, I have found myself doing and saying things like my father. Like him, I am quiet and reserved, not overly expressive of my thoughts and opinions. Interestingly, one of the biggest criticisms I have received over the years is that I should be more vocal and demonstrative. However, that is not my personality.

Tom Newland, the president and CEO of the hospital where I conducted my administrative residency, had served in that position for twenty-five years. He was old school, having been a naval commander before venturing into healthcare. His style was somewhat autocratic, and his military training was very apparent. He was a stickler for protocol, professionalism, dress code, and formality. Those who worked for him knew exactly who was in charge, but there was another side to him that set him apart.

He was genuinely interested in the well-being of his staff. He walked the halls, knew employees by their first names, and ensured his people were cared for. In short, he was compassionate and caring, in some ways contradicting his military background. He was a servant leader when servant leadership wasn't cool.

I worked at that hospital for seven and a half years, including a one-year administrative residency. Over time, I found myself modeling his style. I have dealt with issues and people the way he would have dealt with them, and my leadership style evolved to be much like his. In essence, his compassionate style of leadership, coupled with the mild-mannered personality I inherited from my father, characterizes my leadership style. I believe that this unique blend served me well throughout my career. It provided a strong foundation of leadership built on fundamental principles such as respect, integrity, and compassion.

THE LESSON OF THE CURVEBALL

I have reflected many times on that crucial job-interview experience early in my career. Aside from the disappointment of not getting the job, the experience taught me many valuable lessons. It taught me the importance of being prepared and focused but always on guard for the unanticipated surprise curveball.

It made me more self-aware of my personality and leadership style and how they might influence others. Everyone has a unique personality and style, and it is essential to find the right balance.

Most importantly, it made me much more aware of the importance of sound leadership and the impact a leader has on an organization, especially in healthcare, where the health and well-being of other people are at stake.

COMPASSIONATE LEADERSHIP

My key takeaway from the entire curveball experience is more than being prepared for the unexpected. I promised myself that when the day came when I would be thinking about throwing a nasty curve to a prospective employee, I might say, in advance, with compassion, "Are you ready for a tough one?" Good leaders help their players get set up for the curve.

CHAPTER 2

UNTIL THE HAY IS IN THE BARN

> *How you choose to spend your time is a matter of priorities.*
>
> *Our work isn't done until the hay is in the barn.*

ummertime in Louisiana is hot—very hot—and humid. Typically, there are weeks and months when the temperatures are consistently in the nineties with 95 percent humidity. It can be brutal, especially for outdoor occupations such as farming. The daily work and chores to keep a farm going require true dedication. Farmers must possess the right mindset, a relentless work ethic, and good judgment, the same qualities noted by Ray Brown.

My frame of reference goes back to the mid-1960s, when I was in high school and thinking about my future. I was raised on a farm on the outskirts of a small town in Louisiana. It was a much simpler time, like depicted on the old Andy Griffith television show. We certainly didn't have the level of technological noise we experience today. Most of my summer days were spent doing assigned chores and whatever work was needed on the farm. Everything else was secondary except Sundays, reserved for church, rest, and family activities.

Our family was middle class. My grandfather purchased the farm just after the Great Depression in the early 1930s and sacrificed more than I can imagine to provide for his family. My dad, the oldest of five children, had a similar mindset and commitment. His priorities, like my grandfather's, were his family and faith.

Among other admirable qualities, their work ethic was their most impressive asset. Both my grandfather and my father had full-time jobs at the Standard Oil refinery (known today as ExxonMobil) in Baton Rouge, just twenty miles away. Employment at the refinery provided a steady income and benefits to ensure that their families' basic needs were met.

However, the forty-plus hours at the refinery represented only a fraction of their work in any given week. Once their shift was over at the refinery, the rest of the day was spent on the farm. In my dad's case, he also carved out time to take night classes at LSU to earn his bachelor's degree and to attend weekly drills as a member of the US Army Reserve. He was also a dedicated leader in our local church and a devoted husband to my mother, and he helped raise three children. I can't begin to fathom how he managed his time.

I came along at a time when our country was experiencing tumultuous times. Anyone who is a child of the sixties can relate—my high school years spanned 1965–1969, just as the Vietnam War was escalating and political tensions were at a high pitch.

Each night on the national news, there were reports of war protests, violence, and racial unrest. There was a growing antiwar sentiment and an equally strong peace movement. Flower power, Woodstock, and "Make love, not war" were promoted as alternatives. I was constantly bombarded with confusing messages; however,

I remained focused on my tasks and knew that as long as I was in school and living under my parents' roof, I was somewhat sheltered from the events of the world.

Despite all the external influences, my essential priorities didn't change. I remained focused on academics during the school year and dedicated to my responsibilities on the farm during the summertime. During those summer months, the importance of developing a solid work ethic was etched into my brain. Despite the heat and humidity, the work on the farm was of utmost priority.

For the most part, work on the farm was predictable. There were animals to feed, equipment and fences to maintain, and crops to plant, tend to, or harvest. There was a yearly cycle of what needed to be done through the various seasons.

On our farm, one priority was to grow hay to feed cows during the wintertime and store a little extra to sell to our neighbors. The timing of soil preparation and planting was critical. In the springtime, the appropriate ratio of seed and fertilizer and just the right amount of rainfall provided the foundation for the crops to be reaped later in the year. Too much rain led to flooding, erosion, and drainage issues. Too little rainfall meant that the anticipated yield would be compromised.

The most critical step was the harvesting of crops. In the case of hay, that began about midsummer and lasted well into early fall, the hottest and most humid months of the year. A critical decision point also came into play, and that decision rested with my grandfather. He would consult his *Farmer's Almanac* and watch the local television weather forecast to determine the right day to cut hay. Ideally, hay was cut during days in which little, if any, rain was in the forecast. Once cut, it needed to lie on the ground until dried enough to be raked into windrows. Assuming the weather cooperated, the baling process could proceed. That was when the real work began.

When I was about ten, I was assigned to a team of workers and other family members to do my part. Driving the tractor that pulled the trailer where the bales were loaded and stacked was one of my earliest responsibilities. My dad would put the tractor into gear, get it moving, and then turn the steering wheel over to me. My job was to keep the tractor moving in the right direction and avoid rough spots in the hayfield. As I grew older, I turned that job over to my younger sister, and I was reassigned to stacking bales on the trailer as other workers lifted them from the ground.

As much as I envisioned myself as important as the other "grown-ups" on the work crew, my job involved manual labor. The older I got and the bigger and stronger I grew, the more demanding the manual part of the job became. I could no longer drive the tractor or stack hay on the trailer. I was reassigned to walking on the ground, lifting individual hay bales, and hoisting them onto the trailer as it passed. Once one bale was loaded safely on the trailer, I walked to the next. There was no time for rest in between bales. The tractor never stopped, and I was expected to keep pace.

It didn't take long for the Louisiana heat and humidity to take their toll, but we didn't have the luxury of doing things on our terms. The work needed to be done irrespective of the weather conditions.

My grandfather was old school in his approach to work. Each fifty-pound bale of hay needed to be loaded and stacked on the trailer, hauled to the barn, unloaded, and stacked from the floor to the rafters. While there may have been more-efficient ways to haul hay, he wasn't open to them. He had his ways of doing things, and he was in charge.

Occasionally, he would allow a brief break from the heat by stopping under a large shade tree for a refreshing drink of ice water. But to call it "ice water" was a bit of a stretch. We shared water from a common mason jar my grandmother had filled with ice and water earlier in the day. The jar was wrapped in one, maybe two, brown paper bags, along with a few folded paper cups. Whatever ice was in the jar was long gone within an hour.

A WAKE-UP CALL

Over time, I started to resent my lot in life. It wasn't that I didn't appreciate the importance of hard work or that I disliked farm life. I just felt the calling of something different. As a young and somewhat self-centered teenager, I also developed a case of self-pity.

I spent my summer days working on the farm while my friends played baseball, swam at the community pool, or spent afternoons on the lake. There were days when I was invited to go to a movie or a party at one of my friend's homes, but I was stuck in the middle of a hot and humid hayfield.

I started to vocalize my pent-up resentment more than I probably should have. I began asking to leave early on days when other activities looked more fun and appealing. Some days, I even asked off for an entire day to hang out with my friends. But there was still work to be done, and there were no time clocks in the hayfield. Quitting time wasn't always 4:30 or 5:00, or even dark, especially if there was rain in the forecast.

One afternoon, my grandfather looked me in the eye and delivered one of the most poignant messages, which became an important wake-up call. I can still remember his words as they flowed through my ears and pierced my heart:

How you choose to spend your time is a matter of priorities.
Our work isn't done until the hay is in the barn.

At that moment, I learned several important lessons about dedication and commitment. I knew that there would be times in my life that required making difficult decisions, and sometimes I would be faced with choosing between competing priorities. I also learned that my commitment to a job, whether in the hayfield or anywhere else, would require that I stay true to that commitment. And most importantly, I learned the importance of developing a solid work ethic. Long hours were commonplace on the farm. I didn't know it yet, but long hours would also be commonplace in healthcare.

FIRST PAYCHECK

In the summer of 1968, before I began my senior year of high school, I started getting more serious about my future. One thing was certain: I didn't want to spend the rest of my life hauling hay in Louisiana during the summer. I also knew that a college education would be one of my immediate goals. After all, according to my high school teachers, I would make a great doctor.

As an incentive, attending college would also allow me to qualify for a Selective Service System 2-S student deferment. I would have been proud and willing to serve my country through military service; however, the divisiveness and politics of the Vietnam War during that period were very confusing.

As I previously shared, one of my best friend's fathers was the administrator of our local community hospital. Because of our friendship and my budding interest in medicine, I was hired that summer to work as an orderly in the nursing home connected to the hospital.

It would be my first real job, outside of work on the farm. It was the first time I could recall punching a time clock and getting an actual paycheck made out to me personally. Working in the nursing home gave me a whole new perspective on life. It exposed me to a different environment and opened my eyes to a new set of societal issues. Ironically, the same lessons I had learned on the farm applied to long-term care.

Work performed in a healthcare setting also requires the right mindset, a relentless work ethic, and good judgment. I also learned that the work didn't always fit nicely into an eight-hour shift. The most notable difference was that I got to work indoors in an air-conditioned environment. No longer did I have to endure Louisiana's heat and humidity.

Before I give the impression that I completely abandoned my farm background and ventured down a different path, the summer nursing home job was part time, so my responsibilities on the farm continued as usual. Many days, I would work all morning on the farm, stop at lunchtime, then shower and clean up to make it to my nursing home job. In retrospect, that taught discipline.

Perhaps the most significant lasting impression I recall while working in the nursing home was the dedication of healthcare workers. That was my first real exposure to healthcare other than what I had picked up by watching TV shows like *Marcus Welby, M.D.*, *Ben Casey*, and *Dr. Kildare*.

The passion and dedication of the nursing home staff made an impression on me. I learned that it took a team to deliver healthcare services. Granted, it wasn't in the main hospital, but the nursing home provided an important service, nevertheless. For those brief months, I felt I was on a championship team.

Although my job was at the bottom of the ladder, I took my responsibilities seriously. The work I performed was anything but glamorous. I became proficient at emptying bedpans, changing beds, giving baths, mopping floors, emptying trash, and feeding meals.

I may not have been lifting and stacking fifty-pound hay bales, but the work was just as demanding. In addition to developing a sense of appreciation for the team of healthcare professionals, that summer job also served as an incentive to pursue a healthcare career.

THE HUMAN TOUCH

I have been fortunate to work in healthcare during a very dynamic era. Over my forty-seven-year career, I witnessed fundamental changes in the healthcare system—everything from complex reimbursement methodologies to new clinical and information technologies, a shift from inpatient to outpatient care, and governmental attempts at healthcare reform.

When I walk into a hospital today, I feel an immediate emotion. The environment is significantly different from what it was in 1976 when I began my healthcare administration career, and from what it was during that summer of 1968.

The entire healthcare system has significantly improved how medical services are provided. Technological advances have fundamentally changed how care is delivered, but the human touch remains constant.

During that summer of 1968, I was, for the most part, just an observer. My job required some basic orientation and training, but it didn't require special licensure or certification. Pretty much anyone could do it. As much as anything, the experience provided an appreciation for how people cared for each other. Granted, the team of professionals needed in a nursing home is not nearly as complex as that of a hospital, but teamwork and dedication were just as essential. It takes a special person to work in a geriatric ward.

On most days, the work in a nursing home is routine. Meals are served at the same time, and meds are administered on a predictable schedule. Bedtime for most residents was the same every day, and the time they awakened each morning didn't vary but a few minutes either way.

My duties as an orderly were fairly regimented from when I clocked in until I clocked out. The team seemed to adjust on those rare occasions when the routine changed. Inevitably, there were times when medical conditions might change at a minute's notice. Such is the care for the elderly population. If those situations arose toward the end of a shift, there was no bickering or task avoidance. Everyone pitched in to do their part.

LESSONS FROM THE FARM

The year 1968 is widely known as a tumultuous time in American history. There was a general sense of uneasiness across the nation. The assassinations of Dr. Martin Luther King Jr. and Robert F. Kennedy come readily to mind. The escalation of the Vietnam War and racial unrest led to protests across college campuses. Riots at the Democratic National Convention even marred the presidential election.

For me, however, the issues were more basic. I look back on that summer as a transformational point in my life. The life lessons I had learned on the farm were used in other ways. I knew the importance of working on a team and doing my part. I learned discipline in managing my time, getting to work on time, and performing my duties to the best of my abilities. On those rare occasions when I was asked to work overtime, I learned the importance of having a good work ethic, and those lessons have stayed with me throughout my professional career.

The summer of 1968 will forever be etched in my memory, and I will always be grateful for the experience. I can't say I made any significant contributions besides completing my assigned tasks. But the most important lesson I learned was the same lesson I had learned working on the farm. "The work isn't done until the hay is in the barn."

COMPASSIONATE LEADERSHIP

A friend once observed that living on a farm is a lifelong lesson in compassion. I could write chapters on what I learned, taking on that hard work early in my life. But mostly, I guess, I learned thankfulness. There is *always* something to be thankful for. Good weather, successful births of baby animals, successful harvests, exhaustion at the end of a good workday. I think this kind of challenging experience builds up your empathy for others and allows you to identify with those on your team who are giving more than they might be expected to give.

CHAPTER 3

THE EYES OF THE CONSUMER

> *Sometimes in your career, you will feel pressure when dealing with complex issues. That comes with the territory. But be mindful that others will notice your demeanor, which could easily convey the wrong message.*

My introduction to healthcare may be unique to me, although probably not that much different from others who have ventured down similar paths. Those early experiences working as a nursing home orderly and later as a respiratory therapist provided the road map that eventually led to a four-decade life in healthcare administration. I credit those part-time jobs during high school and college for planting seeds. I'm sure that others have had comparable experiences.

As I was nearing the completion of my master's degree in microbiology at LSU, I decided to change direction and pursue a career in healthcare administration. Several people I respected offered me advice, and the consensus was that I had the necessary intellect and people skills to be successful.

I applied and was accepted into the graduate program in hospital and health administration at UAB. I defended my thesis for a master's degree in microbiology from LSU in August of 1975, then started work on a second master's degree just a few weeks later. I had no time to rest, but I felt a renewed sense of energy and enthusiasm.

The UAB graduate program required a two-year commitment. The first year was spent on campus, completing full-time coursework. I finished all coursework with a perfect straight-A average, which helped me build confidence.

The second year was a more practical experience as an administrative resident in a hospital. I went through the residency interview process with an open mind, but I was leaning toward returning to my home state of Louisiana. However, the residency matching process took me in an entirely different direction.

I interviewed at three different hospitals: one in Alabama, one in Mississippi, and one in Tennessee. The hospital in Alabama was in Birmingham, so staying in Birmingham would have been an easy transition. The opportunity in Mississippi would have taken me closer to home, but I couldn't get comfortable with the limited experience at that particular hospital.

There was something about Tennessee that caught my eye. I knew little about Tennessee other than fond memories of a family vacation to the Smoky Mountains as a child. Fort Sanders Regional Medical Center in Knoxville (known then as Fort Sanders Presbyterian Hospital) was a well-established, respected hospital with a distinguished history.

It was licensed for 535 acute beds but had just received approval to add another 40 inpatient rehabilitation beds. The residency opportunity would provide exposure to a variety of specialty programs and services in a tertiary care setting.

I drove to Knoxville for my interview in early spring, one of the most beautiful times of the year in East Tennessee. Trees and flowers were blooming, the climate was moderate, and the views of the Smoky Mountains were breathtaking. The hospital, the city, and the location had everything I was looking for. So, after my year on campus at UAB, I loaded up my U-Haul and moved to Tennessee, taking me farther from home.

RESIDENCY PROJECT #1

I began my residency on Labor Day weekend, 1976. My first project assignment was to observe the flow of patients in the emergency department over the holiday weekend. It was the unofficial end of summer, and people were out and about, enjoying those last few days of warm weather. Unfortunately, that also meant a higher rate of accidents.

Therefore, the number of patients presenting to the emergency department was higher than usual, resulting in longer wait times, backlogs, and short tempers. Interestingly, this was not atypical of the healthcare delivery system during that era. Hospitals had yet to learn to adjust well to seasonal increases or decreases in volume.

Throughout the weekend, I became very attached to my yellow legal pad, on which I recorded a long list of observations and copious notes. I was not an efficiency expert and had no real expertise. In many respects, I looked at the flawed processes through a healthcare consumer's eyes, not from a healthcare professional's perspective. Nevertheless, it was evident to me that there were many opportunities for improvement.

The registration process, the prioritization of patient acuity, the staffing model, and the inefficiencies of ancillary services created inherent logjams. Yet, with my limited experience and lack of understanding of the system, I could only note my observations. I didn't feel qualified to offer solutions.

By the end of the weekend, I was exhausted after spending most of my waking hours in the emergency department, but the experience was eye-opening. That weekend set the tone for a year of similar learning experiences, which, after all, was the primary intent of the administrative residency.

My year of residency consisted of departmental rotations, meetings, and project assignments much like that weekend project in the emergency department. As much as anything, however, it was an introduction to the US healthcare system of the 1970s. It also allowed me to correlate the graduate program's didactic coursework with real-life experiences. In some cases, the book learning aligned with real life, but the two were often very different. Yet that was part of the learning process, and I found it to be extremely valuable.

A STEP BACK IN TIME

The healthcare delivery model in the 1970s was very different from today. It was an inpatient-dominated system. Most surgical procedures were performed in the hospital operating room. Ancillary services, such as lab and X-ray, were also done in the hospital. It wasn't uncommon for patients to be admitted to the hospital for tests requiring a two- or three-day stay.

I experienced this myself when, in my midtwenties, I developed symptoms of numbness in my extremities. My doctor, a neurosurgeon, admitted me for a battery of tests over three days. Truth be known, I didn't require much in the way of nursing care. I was mobile and self-sufficient. An interesting aspect of that hospital admission was that my health insurance required an inpatient admission to pay the claim. Such would be unheard of today. In today's world, the incentives would be just the opposite: do as much as possible on an outpatient basis.

I also had the opportunity to observe the work ethic of physicians and developed a deep respect for the medical profession. Doctors were at the hospital all hours of the day and night. Their dedication and perseverance brought back memories of my grandfather working long hours on the farm, not quitting until the hay was in the barn. Back then, physicians of every specialty were required by the medical staff bylaws to take their fair share of emergency call rotation, and they gladly complied.

Attending to patients in the emergency department was one way to build their practice, and being available for emergencies was considered significant value. Physicians would admit patients and make rounds twice daily to check on them. Today's incentives are much different. Physicians generally expect to be compensated for taking emergency calls, and hospitalists attend to inpatients. The paradigm has undoubtedly shifted.

The surgery schedule on Mondays was extremely long. There were also patients admitted for tests, meaning that admissions to the hospital on Sundays were much higher than on other days of the week. Patients and their families started arriving midafternoon every Sunday.

Part of the Sunday-afternoon routine called for someone to set out additional chairs in the hospital lobby to accommodate the number of people waiting to be admitted. Hospital employees jokingly compared the hospital lobby to a Greyhound bus station. People were everywhere: standing, sitting, and leaning against walls.

The admissions process was slow and laborious. There was no preadmission registration. All information needed to admit a patient was gathered during the on-site admission process. The hospital had a computer system, which was very primitive compared to today's information systems. It was primarily programmed to document patient demographics, charges, and insurance information. Clinical records were still paper based.

Observing and evaluating the admissions process and looking for ways to be more efficient became my residency project #2. For several months, my Sunday afternoons were spent in the admitting office, taking notes and making observations.

Such was the life of an administrative resident. I was there to learn and observe. I was assigned countless projects that no one else wanted to do. But that was part of the experience.

As a resident, I was looked upon as a student, which was technically correct since I had not yet earned my degree. I was free to roam around the hospital and go in and out of hospital departments in a nonthreatening manner. I was no one's boss. As much as anything, I was everyone's peer. I could ask questions without fear of repercussion. It was a gratifying experience.

A CHANGE IN PERCEPTION

Following my residency, how people perceived me changed drastically. I had completed all academic requirements, including successfully defending my thesis, and was ready for full-time employment. However, I hadn't been given much guidance or advice on how to look for a job, so I was left to my own devices.

By the end of my residency, however, Knoxville started to feel like home. I grew to love the community and developed loyalty to the hospital. I liked the people and the culture, and I was excited about the hospital's future.

As fate would have it, the most promising job was right before me. Fort Sanders approached me about staying in a yet-to-be-defined administrative role. A major multistory construction project had been planned to accommodate the additional rehabilitation beds and to expand space for other departments. The job proposal was to help coordinate the move into the new patient tower. That sounded interesting, and since I had no other real job opportunities, I gladly accepted the offer. It was an entry-level administrative position, but I was eager to start.

I hadn't anticipated what would happen next. Once I became a full-time administrative staff member, I was no longer looked upon as a student. I was no longer considered a peer. I was no longer "Jim."

Overnight, I became "Mr. Decker" and had a perceived level of authority and executive standing. Even though I was in an entry-level staff position with limited authority and no direct reports, I was viewed differently by the hospital staff. It was a real wake-up call for me to make that transition.

I even struggled somewhat with how I viewed myself. I was the same person I had always been, but now I was in a new role. As much as I wanted to enjoy the excitement of my "promotion," I still missed the days of being one of the gang. But those days were behind me, and I needed to move on. Being called "Mr. Decker" didn't sound quite right, yet the page had been turned. In the blink of an eye, I had moved to the other side of the table.

I spent the next several months focused on my new responsibilities. My daily routine was self-directed because I was in a somewhat ill-defined role. I had to be creative in determining what needed to be done and developing a plan of action to make it happen. It required coordinating many moving pieces and interacting with various hospital staff, which proved beneficial. I had to develop trust with everyone to let them see I wasn't going to start throwing around my administrative power suddenly. I had not changed as a person; I had just changed roles.

AN OFFICE IN THE SAME ZIP CODE AS THE C-SUITE

Administrative residents are at the bottom of the food chain. Not only do they have no absolute authority or organizational standing, but they also have slim pickings regarding office space. At least, that was my experience.

When I began my residency in the fall of 1976, my office was nowhere near the main executive suite. I'm not sure it was even in the same zip code. I was assigned a small cubbyhole near the nurses' station on the third floor that had previously been a storage closet. About a week before I started, the third-floor staff was asked to clean out the closet and make room for a "student administrator."

A small desk, a half-broken chair, a used bookshelf, and a telephone magically transformed that closet into a usable office. It wasn't fancy, but I was happy to have something to call my own ... for about three weeks.

Over the next seven and a half years, I occupied six different offices. Any time space needs changed, so did the location of my office. When I transitioned into a full-time role, I was granted a more prominent, private office. While it still wasn't in the main executive suite, it was a step closer. I put down some roots, adding new furniture and artwork to personalize my space.

After eighteen months in that initial entry-level job, I was promoted to vice president and moved into the C-suite. As nice as the new office was, the reality of being in the line of fire set in. I quickly learned that having an office in a different zip code may not have been so bad after all.

DIVIDED LOYALTIES

Once promoted to vice president, I started calling Knoxville home. I became active in several local organizations and took time to learn about the rich history of the community. One of the more notable historical events occurred on the hill where the hospital is located. During the Civil War, Knoxville was a city with divided loyalties. Because of its geographic location, both Union and Confederate loyalists were living in the region. Fort Sanders was a Union outpost that was very strategic because of its location. The mountains, farmland, road system, railways, and Tennessee River were essential to Union and Confederate troops. Some referred to Knoxville as the "Arch of the Confederacy."

On November 29, 1863, the Battle of Fort Sanders was fought on the hillside where the Union outpost was located. The battle itself may be somewhat nondescript compared to other, more famous Civil War battles; however, it proved to be a pivotal battle that had a long-lasting impact on the entire region.

Although the battle lasted only about twenty minutes, the Union victory solidified control of valuable supply channels and transportation along the Tennessee River, which runs through Knoxville.

I am not a Civil War historian, but I credit Dr. Digby Seymour, then an anesthesiologist at Fort Sanders Regional Medical Center, for prompting my interest in the Battle of Fort Sanders. In addition to being a well-respected physician, he was a skilled author. His book, *Divided Loyalties*,[11] provides excellent insight into the Battle of Fort Sanders and other facts about the region's history. I was honored when he gave me a personalized signed copy of his book.

Little did I know that I would also be living in Knoxville during another significant historical event when, in 1982, the world came to Knoxville. Through the vision and leadership of several community leaders, Knoxville was selected to host the 1982 World's Fair. What began as an energy exposition grew in scope and met the criteria to be deemed a World's Fair.

As expected, there were mixed feelings about the fair throughout the community. Indeed, there was excitement with the opportunity to put Knoxville on the map and attract exhibits from countries worldwide. However, there was also apprehension about more practical issues such as traffic congestion, lodging availability, and other logistical concerns. From my perspective, I thought it was great. I was excited that such a significant event was happening in our community.

My girlfriend (soon-to-be fiancée) and I bought season passes and enjoyed everything the fair offered. We were among the thousands who attended the opening ceremonies when President Ronald Reagan made the official proclamation to open the fair, and attendees were entertained by one of Tennessee's most beloved singers, Dinah Shore.

The senior executive team at the hospital shared the concerns regarding traffic congestion and logistics. We didn't know what to expect, so we planned to operate as usual during those six months, even though the hospital was only eight blocks from the fair site. In the months leading up to opening day, one of our primary concerns was transportation around town. We feared traffic jams throughout the city, making it hard to get to and from the hospital campus.

---

11   Digby G. Seymour, *Divided Loyalties* (The East Tennessee Historical Society, 1982).

The main concern was patient transportation, especially during emergencies. Another more practical concern was the need for routine deliveries of supplies, clinical specimens, and other critical items. Our solution was to purchase a motorbike (a 1982 moped) if normal transportation was backed up. As it turned out, our fears never really materialized.

Indeed, there were days when traffic was heavier than usual, but those days were relatively infrequent. The best use of that moped was for a purpose that wasn't intended. It became a handy mode of transportation at lunchtime when I would ride those eight blocks to the fair, use my season pass to gain entry, and spend my lunch hour wandering around the fairgrounds. I used that opportunity to visit exhibits from other countries and sample unique food items. As I recall, the Chinese, Australian, and American pavilions were the most popular.

Fort Sanders Regional Medical Center also used the fair to gain visibility and provide a valuable service to fair visitors. The hospital was granted space at the fair to erect a tent that became a central location to distribute health and wellness materials and provide basic health screenings. It also served as an excellent shelter from the summertime heat and humidity. The tent wasn't intended to provide first aid and wasn't equipped or staffed to deal with medical emergencies. Its primary purpose was health promotion and education, and it was staffed by student nurses from the hospital's school of nursing.

EARLY LESSONS

When I was appointed vice president, I was twenty-seven years old and still very green around the ears. For the first time, I had departments reporting directly to me, and in some cases, the department heads were years my senior. But I saw it as an opportunity to use the lessons

I had learned up to that point. Some lessons resulted from personal accomplishments, others from mistakes and poor judgment. Yet I learned that both types of lessons proved to be extremely valuable.

Managing people older than me posed several interesting challenges, but it also proved to be a worthwhile experience. At first, there was a period of cat and mouse. I could sense they were watching and waiting to see what this young hotshot would do. For some, I sensed they were also waiting for me to fail. Although they never really verbalized directly to me, I am sure there was also some pent-up resentment. After all, most of them had been in their respective positions longer than I had even been out of school. Who was I to tell them what to do?

I worked hard to gain their trust and prove that I was qualified for the position. Over time, I felt that I succeeded, but it certainly wasn't easy. The most challenging task was the annual performance reviews of direct reports, which I didn't enjoy.

As a relatively young executive, I had not yet mastered evaluating others' performance, but I tried to be balanced and fair in my assessments. I identified areas where they performed well and areas that needed improvement, and I think most appreciated my objective assessment.

One performance review, however, didn't go very well, and it became a very troubling and sensitive issue. A department head had been in a management position for over twenty-five years. This individual had made tremendous contributions to the organization and was from a prominent and respected family. However, I felt that interpersonal relationships with peer managers needed improvement. I noted these in the performance appraisal, along with a list of accomplishments and positive qualities.

But it was not well accepted. There was defensiveness and resentment. Rather than take my appraisal constructively, this manager became belligerent. After a few sarcastic comments about my age and inexperience, this individual stormed out of my office and demanded a meeting with my boss.

I was taken aback. Of all the managers who reported to me, this person was the only one with that reaction. After gaining my composure, I sought out my boss to get his advice. He wasn't immediately available but told me he would adjust his schedule to meet with me before the end of the day. When we finally met, he had already heard from the disgruntled department head and was anxious to listen to my side of the story.

My meeting with him was a significant turning point. I marveled at his composure and objectivity in assessing the situation. He understood the reasoning behind the issues I had noted in the appraisal. Not only did he support me, but he took it upon himself to schedule a meeting with everyone involved.

How he handled this issue was a thing of beauty. It was a lesson in objectivity, fairness, and decisiveness. As much as anything, it was another wake-up call. I had the title and organizational authority but had not yet fully earned my stripes. It took the CEO, with greater authority, to diffuse the issue. That taught me an important lesson.

Although that situation was very stressful and challenging, the relationships with all other direct reports were positive. While there were some rough spots along the way, trust and mutual respect improved over time. I tried hard to prove myself worthy of my position.

One happy moment broke the ice for me. I had been in the vice president position for about two years when I reached my thirtieth birthday. That was a major milestone, but not one that I broadcast throughout the organization. Somehow, however, birthdays have a way of spreading through the grapevine.

As fate would have it, my birthday fell on the day I had my regularly scheduled monthly meeting with my direct reports. We got through a routine agenda and were ready for adjournment when I was surprised with a flurry of balloons, streamers, noisemakers, and my favorite cake—chocolate devil's food with chocolate icing. Accompanied by one department head who played the guitar, I was serenaded with the customary "Happy Birthday." They also presented me with a lovely clock for my desk. That clock has made its way to my desk at every stop in my career.

The most valuable lessons were those I learned by observing others. As mentioned earlier in this book, my mentor and first real role model was very formal in his style. But he was also a very compassionate leader. I learned a lot from watching how he dealt with issues and people. Because of his military background, he was very structured and professional but also very genuine and highly respected. I aspired to model my career similarly and build that same type of respect among people with whom I interacted.

As I look back on those early leadership lessons, however, I am cognizant of how things have changed over time. My mentor was a stickler for professional protocol. Male executive team members were always expected to wear a coat and tie at work, including Saturdays and Sundays. We were allowed to remove our coats in our office, or once we got to our car, but a coat was to be worn whenever we walked the hospital halls.

He had two other requirements that would seem outlandish in today's world. For men, no facial hair was permitted, other than a mustache, if the mustache didn't extend below the upper lip. Nurses were required to dress in all-white uniforms, including the traditional nurse's cap and white shoes. I shudder to think what his opinion would be of today's dress codes.

It also became apparent that if I were ever to be considered for a promotion, I had to adopt the work ethic that was expected. This included arriving at the office before the boss arrived and not leaving until after he was gone for the day. This was an unwritten rule that I picked up along the way, but I have since learned that it is also true in many other organizations.

In those days, an intercom system allowed instant communication between all executive offices. I recall many times when my boss would buzz me on the intercom and ask, "Jim, are you busy?" I froze up the first few times this happened, not knowing how to respond. If I said, "No, I'm not busy," what message would that convey? If I said, "Yes, I am busy," it might give the impression that what he needed was less important.

Over time, I learned to respond by saying, "I am currently working on something, but I am at a good stopping point. I'll be right there." Then, I was in his office in less than a minute.

LASTING IMPRESSIONS

I learned several important lessons from my mentor, and these lessons remained with me throughout my career. The first was to stay balanced in my personal life: work hard and stay focused on the job's duties but take time for myself and enjoy leisure activities.

The second lesson came from his intuition that healthcare would experience significant changes in the coming years, requiring doing things differently. He advised that human nature is such that most people inherently resist change, but the same people who resist change will be the loudest to complain if everything remains the same. His advice was to use my best judgment (i.e., what would Ray Brown do?) when implementing change.

The third lesson was even more compelling and hit me right between the eyes. There was a period when I was struggling with a very challenging issue involving some strong and opinionated personalities. A difficult decision weighed heavily on my mind, affecting my demeanor. While walking the halls of the hospital one day, I confronted my boss, who was coming the other way. My head was hanging low, and I was deep in thought. When he asked how everything was going, I mumbled an unconvincing "Okay."

I didn't respond in my usual friendly manner, and he immediately noticed a difference in my demeanor. About a half hour later, he summoned me to his office. Once behind closed doors, he looked me in the eye and delivered these words of advice:

> *Sometimes in your career, you will feel pressure when dealing with complex issues.*
>
> *That comes with the territory. But be mindful that others will notice your demeanor, and it could easily convey the wrong message.*

It was only the beginning of a career filled with difficult decisions, most of which were much more complex than that one. In retrospect, that issue would not even rank among the top one hundred most challenging issues I would deal with during my career. I was insulated from real pressure. I was a senior executive but not the most senior executive. There was a sense of comfort knowing I had a boss I could consult when the pressure was too hard to handle.

I would not have that luxury in my next job. Unbeknownst to me at the time, the most difficult decisions I ever had to make were lurking just a few months away.

COMPASSIONATE LEADERSHIP

Now, some forty-seven years later, I look back on that troubling issue through a different lens. At the time, I felt the weight of the world on my shoulders, and I thought that my decisions would alter the course of modern civilization. I couldn't fathom being confronted with a more difficult issue, but I couldn't have been more wrong. Yet I was beginning to learn about feeling compassion for the seriousness of my decisions.

CHAPTER 4

DOWNSIZING LOOMS

> *To this day, that entire process still weighs heavily on my mind. But I knew that it was necessary to preserve the hospital's future. I had done what was expected of me, but I still had a sunken feeling in my stomach. It was a brutal welcome to the world of a CEO.*

My mentor was right. Healthcare was poised for significant changes in the early 1980s. Medicare, especially, was going through a major overhaul. Forecasts of the sustainability of the Medicare program were that it would go broke if something wasn't done to curb increasing healthcare costs. Hospitals were the biggest target.

Since the inception of Medicare in the 1960s, hospitals had been reimbursed based on their costs to care for Medicare patients. Hospitals were paid through biweekly Periodic Interim Payments and then submitted a detailed cost report at the end of their fiscal year. Based on the cost report, there was a reconciliation payment (or payable) to balance the books.

It was a pretty good deal for hospitals since they didn't have to be overly concerned about holding down costs if the federal government reimbursed them based on costs. Eventually, however, that good deal had to come to an end. The federal government could no longer afford it.

CRUCIBLE #1:
THE MEDICARE PROSPECTIVE PAYMENT SYSTEM

The Centers for Medicare and Medicaid Services (CMS) established the Medicare Prospective Payment System (PPS) as a provision within the Social Security Amendments of 1983. Explicitly intended to address expensive hospital care, PPS is a payment methodology that prospectively determines the financial reimbursement to hospitals for care provided to Medicare patients. Based on the patient's diagnosis and other contributing factors, a predetermined rate is reimbursed to the hospital, regardless of the intensity of services provided. The premise of PPS was to incentivize hospitals to control costs.[12]

The Medicare Prospective Payment System (PPS) was introduced and became effective in 1983. This fundamentally changed the way that hospitals were reimbursed. Under the new system, hospitals would be paid based on a multivariable formula related to individual patient diagnoses. The Diagnosis-Related Group (DRG) reimbursement methodology became the law of the land.

---

12   American Hospital Directory (AHD), accessed July 29, 2024, https://www.ahd.com/ip_ipps08.html.

This forced hospitals to pay much closer attention to controlling costs. Since the DRG payment was prospectively determined per the formula, hospitals were no longer guaranteed to be reimbursed their full costs. Efficient hospitals were rewarded for controlling costs, while inefficient hospitals were penalized. In response, hospitals revamped their accounting departments, added cost accountants to their staff, and looked for ways to become more efficient.

The enactment of PPS got my attention. I recognized that I needed to expand my knowledge of finance, economics, and accounting. The UAB master's in hospital and health administration program was highly regarded, and I was confident that I had a solid foundation in healthcare administration. However, the program didn't emphasize other key aspects of general business.

Suddenly, I felt ill-prepared for the challenges lurking ahead. I remember sitting in my office one day thinking about the future of healthcare and what I should do to be better prepared. A newly published book by John Naisbitt entitled *Megatrends*[13] also encouraged me to take notice of more broad changes in the US economy that could potentially affect healthcare. My comfort zone began to feel uneasy.

Just a few blocks away from the hospital was the University of Tennessee (UT), which offered a full array of undergraduate and graduate programs, one of which was a master of business administration (MBA). At that time, UT offered a part-time MBA program where students could take a few courses each quarter.

As a bonus, Fort Sanders had an employee tuition-reimbursement program. I didn't want to miss such a golden opportunity to expand my knowledge, so I enrolled in the MBA program and began

---

13   John Naisbitt, *Megatrends* (Warner Books, 1982).

taking night classes. If things went as planned, I could earn my MBA within a few years.

One course I took while working on my MBA focused on emerging business trends. My professor assigned a reading list of newly released books, all hot off the press. The book that made the biggest impression on me was *In Search of Excellence*[14] by Tom Peters and Robert Waterman.

That book became a number one national bestseller, providing great "behind the curtains" insight into some of the most successful American companies. I couldn't help but wonder how, or if, their principles might apply to healthcare. It encouraged me to look at healthcare organizations from a broader perspective.

BLAZING NEW GROUND

My fiancée and I got married on August 27, 1983, my thirty-second birthday. By then, I had become settled in my vice president position and had been given even more operational responsibility. My wife completed her nursing training and accepted a job as a registered nurse in the neonatal intensive care unit at East Tennessee Children's Hospital, just across the street from Fort Sanders. Everything was falling into place.

Then, one day, I received a call from a professional colleague at another hospital in Knoxville. He told me there would be job openings for a CEO position at two hospitals in Middle Tennessee, near Nashville. A long-tenured CEO at one hospital had announced his retirement, while the other opening was due to the resignation of a CEO who had taken another job.

---

14   Thomas J. Peters and Robert H. Waterman, *In Search of Excellence* (Warner Books, 1982).

My friend sensed that I had progressed in my career to a point where a new challenge might interest me. I had been at Fort Sanders for seven and a half years, the last five as vice president. I thanked him for his call and began to process the possibilities. From a professional standpoint, he was right. I needed to consider both opportunities. I could spread my wings and take the next bold step in my career.

That evening, I shared the news with my wife, and she was very supportive. She knew that I should evaluate new opportunities when they arose, even if it meant that we might need to move to another city. So, I updated my résumé, drafted two separate cover letters, and placed them in the mail. Neither hospital was using an executive search firm. In both cases, the hospital boards had formed a CEO search committee. Over the next few months, I had multiple phone conversations and in-person interviews with people at both hospitals. Like any new opportunity, there were pros and cons for both hospitals and both communities, but the opportunity in Gallatin, Tennessee, seemed to be the best fit. We enjoyed our visit there, we liked the people, and we felt comfortable moving there if the position was offered.

And that's exactly what happened. In May 1984, I submitted my notice to Fort Sanders and accepted the position of CEO of Sumner Regional Medical Center, known then as Sumner Memorial Hospital. For a newlywed and relatively inexperienced executive, I was a bit nervous, but I had prepared myself for this moment and was ready for the challenge.

The next few weeks were spent wrapping up loose ends at work, preparing for an orderly transition, and coordinating the logistical aspects of the move. I had mixed emotions. It was hard to leave Fort Sanders and the Knoxville community, but it was exciting to be blazing new ground.

I reported for duty at Sumner Memorial bright and early on the morning of Monday, June 4, 1984. That first week was somewhat of a blur, with much of my time spent meeting people, touring the hospital facilities, and learning my way around town. It was exhausting, but it was a good exhaustion.

The game plan was for me to work for a few weeks alongside the retiring CEO, and then assume the CEO position upon his retirement. Little did I know that the next six months would be some of the most challenging months of my career.

REALITY SETS IN

I began my tenure in Gallatin with great anticipation. I remember setting three professional goals for myself. First, I wanted to develop a track record as a CEO. Granted, I had seven and a half years of experience, but none as CEO.

Sumner Memorial, then licensed for 155 beds, provided the perfect setting for me to gain this experience. It was the only hospital in a community of about 25,000 people and provided a great opportunity to use the knowledge and skills I had gained at Fort Sanders.

My second goal was to finish work on my MBA, but Knoxville was two hundred miles away, so taking courses at UT seemed out of the question. There were other options, but that wasn't my highest immediate priority.

The third goal was to attain my Fellowship in the American College of Health Executives. This was considered the gold-standard credential for all healthcare executives. I had met the prerequisite criteria and had passed the written and oral exams. I just needed to complete my thesis and submit it for approval.

After about a month on the job, reality set in. Two major issues created consternation and soul-searching. The first was something that I had not fully expected. My predecessor was a fine man. He worked at the hospital for over thirty years, the last twenty-five as CEO. He was a native of the area and was well respected in the community. He was extremely helpful in orienting me to the hospital and the community, and I will always appreciate the support he gave me.

But the timing of his retirement was a bit ill-defined. I had accepted the job under the impression that he would retire within a few weeks, maybe as long as a month. But it quickly became obvious to me that his real intentions were otherwise. His retirement date became a moving target, and I wondered when, or if, he intended to turn the reins over to me. My patience was tested, but I used that time to build relationships with physicians, staff, and community leaders. I knew that my time would eventually come.

The more concerning issue was something that I should have anticipated. Despite staying current on healthcare issues, I failed to fully appreciate the impact of PPS. Yes, I had done my homework and had developed the knowledge and understanding of how it would work, but the impact came much faster than I expected. Sumner Memorial's fiscal year ended on May 31, which meant that effective June 1, the hospital was officially under the PPS reimbursement methodology. When I began my job on June 4, the clock was already ticking.

To the hospital's credit, internal systems and processes had been implemented. There was a precertification process to ensure that Medicare patients met admission criteria. There was a utilization review process to monitor services provided to Medicare patients and ensure that length-of-stay requirements were met. There was a dedicated staff member who consulted with physicians regarding patient progress and discharge planning. All these critical activities had been implemented per Medicare guidelines. Medicare's intent was obvious … reduce costs associated with the care of patients by curtailing inappropriate hospital admissions and reducing the length of stay.

If the intended goal of PPS was to decrease the hospital's inpatient census, the intent was successful. Historically, Sumner Memorial had an annual occupancy rate of 90–95 percent, dating back to when it first opened in 1959. The hospital had continuously operated in the black, something the board was very proud of. All of that changed once PPS was enacted. During the first six months under PPS, the hospital census dropped to an average of around 70 percent and recorded a financial loss each month. It was unprecedented in the history of the hospital.

About five months into my tenure, the CEO finally retired. I think he saw a troubling trend developing and thought it would be a good time to bow out. Now the pressure of developing a plan of action to address the financial losses rested on my shoulders. Being a hospital CEO was what I had asked for, but this was not what I had envisioned. I certainly had my work cut out for me.

The first task was to reevaluate the number of staffed beds. Up until then, all 155 beds were needed throughout the year. Granted, there were peaks and valleys, but the full inpatient capacity was justified. Under PPS, however, the number of occupied beds declined.

We analyzed inpatient utilization data to determine the best configuration and concluded that we could close a nursing unit to make the most optimal use of inpatient resources. This would also call for staff downsizing since the current number of personnel would no longer be needed. Here I am, in my first few months on the job, already talking about downsizing, a polite term for layoffs.

Once we had developed our plan to close a nursing unit, the holiday season was quickly approaching. Thanksgiving was right around the corner, and Christmas was just a few weeks away. The last thing I wanted to do was to announce a layoff just before the holidays. Therefore, we decided to wait until after the first of the year to implement our plan. The holiday season that year was not very festive for me. The looming downsizing was always in the back of my mind, and there were many sleepless nights.

The lessons I learned from my mentor during my years at Fort Sanders took on a new meaning. I couldn't help but think about his wisdom and advice. It was one of those times when I knew my down-in-the-dumps demeanor must have been showing.

Although I was agonizing over the action that needed to be taken, I tried, as best I could, to continue to convey a positive attitude. I knew the entire organization looked to me to make decisions in the hospital's best interests, and in my new role as CEO, that came with the territory.

I also started to anticipate the negative reactions that would follow. I remembered those tough decisions that I had to make during my early years at Fort Sanders and how trivial they seemed in comparison.

HAVOC

January 1985 was one of the coldest months ever in Middle Tennessee. We had to deal with multiple heating issues at the hospital because of an aging physical plant, and there were many days when snow and ice made it difficult to get around town. Schools were closed for several days, intermittent electrical outages created havoc with daily routines, and many scheduled activities were canceled. People were on edge. Tempers among staff, patients, and family members were short. It was already an unpleasant set of circumstances. Then, I had the undesirable task of delivering the final blow.

With the backing of the board, our downsizing plan was implemented. We had developed an extensive communications plan, including written memos and in-person employee meetings. The management team and the medical staff leadership were the first to be informed. Then, the announcement was made organization-wide. The scripted message was very detailed as to why such action was necessary. We could no longer support the level of inpatient services we had in the past. We needed to downsize to adjust to the new reality of PPS. The primary message was that a nursing unit would soon be closed.

The downsizing plan was much more delicate to manage. We reviewed the new staffing plan to determine which positions would be affected and had a number in mind, but that was not communicated publicly. We also knew several employees were nearing retirement, so the first wave of downsizing included an early retirement incentive for eligible employees. We reasoned that this would allow employees to make their own decisions. The number of employees laid off could be minimized depending on how many employees took advantage of the incentive. It was a difficult and emotionally exhausting process.

When all was said and done, more employees than anticipated chose to take early retirement, so we only had to lay off a relatively small number.

To this day, that entire process still weighs heavily on my mind. But I knew that it was necessary to preserve the hospital's future. I had done what was expected of me, but I still had a sunken feeling in my stomach. It was a brutal welcome to the world of a CEO.

The closure of the nursing unit and subsequent staff downsizing provided a temporary fix. Adjusting the number of staffed beds brought the hospital operations more in line with anticipated patient demand. Financial performance would take several months to improve because of the inherent costs associated with downsizing, but I felt that we were on track toward stability.

Our attention then turned to the long term. What other uses could we identify for that closed nursing unit? It would take a few more months to figure out, but that question would eventually be answered.

I knew there would be some fallout from the downsizing issue, but I underestimated to what extent. Being the only hospital in a community has some benefits and liabilities. In Gallatin, it didn't help that the hospital was a county-owned facility, placing it in the public spotlight. Everyone, from elected officials to the public, took an interest in what was happening at the hospital, and the local newspaper saw it as an opportunity to generate headlines.

Our communications plan included a news release to the media explaining the reasoning behind our decisions, but those messages seemed to get lost in translation. I made myself available for interviews with the newspaper to provide more background and information, but that only went so far.

Even though the hospital had always enjoyed a generally positive relationship with the press, I think they saw this issue as an opportunity to second-guess our actions. I also believe that the change in hospital leadership factored into the storyline. Never mind that Medicare changed the rules. The public saw that the hospital had a new, young, hotshot CEO, and the hospital was going down the tubes. I was only eight months into my tenure and was already taking heat.

As is true in most small towns, the grapevine has a way of spreading misinformation, and I was an easy target. After all, the hospital had always operated in the black, and the patient census had always been in the 90–95 percent range. The hospital had never resorted to layoffs and the closure of an entire nursing unit. My predecessor had led the hospital through growth and prosperity, including several facility expansion projects.

The prevailing sentiment within the community was "What is this new guy doing to destroy our hospital?"

There were also rumors that the county commission might consider selling the hospital to a for-profit chain. For the first time in my career, I wondered what I had gotten myself into.

I'll admit that there were many moments when I felt like throwing in the towel, but somehow, I remained steadfast and focused. Over the next several months, people started to rally behind me. The hospital board, employees, and medical staff remained supportive. They understood the changes in healthcare and wanted to do whatever was necessary to get us through this difficult time. As expected, our financial performance started improving by the end of the fiscal year in May, and we could turn our attention toward the future.

Through luck or divine intervention, as we started evaluating alternative plans for that closed nursing unit, we were approached by a rehabilitation company looking to lease space for an inpatient rehab program. The size and configuration of our vacant unit met their specifications, so we agreed to the terms of a three-year lease. That development provided the cash flow needed to cover our overhead and gave us more time to develop our long-term plans. I could finally breathe a sigh of relief when those lease payments started flowing in.

THE 25-50-25 RULE

The five years I spent in Gallatin were some of the most gratifying of my professional career. Despite that challenging first year, things began to improve, and we were able to proceed with some long-term strategic initiatives. I worked hard to foster an optimistic outlook for the future, and with time, I slowly gained the support and respect of key constituents. But it was certainly no cakewalk. It took determination and relationship building to overcome the stigma of that first year.

Perhaps the most difficult challenge was convincing those within the hospital walls that I knew what I was doing. The advice about dealing with change that I had gotten from my mentor years before came into play in so many ways. Following someone who had been the CEO for twenty-five years was no easy task. I was reminded, almost daily, of how things had been done differently under his leadership.

I wish I had a dollar for every time someone said "That's not how we do things around here" or "We tried that once before, and it didn't work."

I would estimate that about 25 percent of the hospital staff had that perspective. I eventually got used to those roadblocks and learned to let those negative comments go in one ear and out the other. This was a new day and age in healthcare, and the past was no longer a good predictor of the future.

If 25 percent of the staff were resistant to change, there was another 25 percent on the opposite end of that spectrum. Not only did they like change, but they embraced it. From those in that group, I would get comments such as "I am so glad you changed that. It should have been done twenty years ago."

I took that as an endorsement of what I was trying to accomplish. Still, I also had to pull back the reigns and not move too swiftly without carefully considering all alternatives and unintended consequences. I spent most of my time focusing on the remaining 50 percent.

It was that group that I sensed was open to change but didn't react strongly one way or the other. I felt that if I could get support from 75 percent of the organization, we could do great things together. Over the years, I started referring to that as the *25-50-25* rule.

I also spent time getting involved in the community, yet the stigma of that first year was hard to shake. Like the hospital staff, I had to prove myself to community leaders and the general public and convince them I was qualified for the job. People continued to compare me to my predecessor, and some had reached conclusions about the direction of the hospital without knowing the whole story. I learned that the CEO of the only hospital in town was in a very visible position.

Everyone seemed to know who I was, and I felt all eyes were on me. However, that also created an opportunity to educate them on healthcare issues. I spoke to civic clubs and community groups on a routine basis, mainly to provide information that would help them understand. I made it a priority to be involved in community organizations.

By my third year in Gallatin, I was appointed to the United Way board and elected the Gallatin Chamber of Commerce president. I took that as a compliment and acknowledgment that I had something to contribute.

Four years into my tenure at Sumner, I checked off the three professional goals I had set for myself when I started. I had developed a track record as a CEO, albeit with some bumps along the way. I eventually finished my MBA through independent study and weekly commutes to Knoxville. My ACHE thesis was approved, and I advanced to Fellow in the ACHE.

From a personal standpoint, my wife and I welcomed two children into our family, and our lives began to revolve around them. We had made close friends and were comfortably settled into the Gallatin community. I could envision myself staying there for several more years. But that's not the way the cards were dealt. Another opportunity was waiting in the wings.

COMPASSIONATE LEADERSHIP

Comparing the challenges of a small role in a small hospital with the leadership challenges of the most recent years created a new sense of self for me. I guess I was strengthened by the difficulties yet weakened by the not-automatic acceptance of my wisdom and acumen. And the gold in all that ... was that I began to feel real compassion for myself. I need to make that point clear. It is much easier to develop and nurture a compassionate, empathetic leadership style after discovering compassion for yourself.

CHAPTER 5

BUSINESS (NOT) AS USUAL

In my view, healthcare is a sacred mission.

Nothing can replace the value of learning by doing. That was certainly true during those first few years in Gallatin when I went through my own on-the-job training. There was no way around it being my first CEO job, and I was still a little green behind my ears. I quickly learned that the community and key constituents were looking to me to lead the organization by exercising good judgment and making decisions that were in the hospital's best interests.

As might be expected, there were decisions that I felt good about, yet there were others that I would like to have back. Sometimes, twenty-twenty hindsight can shed new light on a situation or provide additional information unavailable at the time. I considered those as teaching moments that would benefit me down the road.

The most important lesson I learned during those early years was staying focused. In sports, it is akin to keeping your eye on the ball and being prepared for the unexpected. I learned that complacency is unacceptable and can easily be the first step toward failure. This is especially true in a dynamic environment such as healthcare, which is fast paced and ever changing.

I remember one of my professors at UAB describing the role of a healthcare executive as that of a "change agent." He believes successful hospital CEOs don't just deal with change; they lead it. They are never satisfied with the status quo. He went so far as to say that people who are averse to change should choose a profession other than healthcare. Like it or not, healthcare is continually evolving, and the CEO's role is to manage that change.

THE EVOLUTION OF MANAGED CARE

CRUCIBLE #2:

MANAGED CARE

The term "managed care" describes an approach to health-care that focuses on reducing costs while maintaining a high quality of care. Common features include restricted provider networks, strict oversight of services rendered, limited access to specialty care, and prescription drug tiers. Health maintenance organizations (HMOs) and preferred provider organizations (PPOs) are examples of early managed care models.[15]

When I thought things were running smoothly in Gallatin, the next big wave of change suddenly emerged. Almost overnight, and on

---

15   Healthcare.gov, accessed July 29, 2024, https://www.healthcare.gov/choose-a-plan/.

the heels of PPS, US healthcare was introduced to a new term that would soon become a part of our everyday vocabulary. "Managed care" dominated our attention, as did several other alphabet-soup terms such as "MCO," "HMO," "PPO," "PHO," and "IPA."

Efforts to curb the growth of healthcare costs had migrated from the federal government to the private sector, and corporate America and private healthcare insurers were embracing the same focus on cost control. This affected the relationships between hospitals and commercial insurance companies, as well as the relationships between insurance companies and major employers.

Hospitals renegotiated contracts with insurance companies, yet they had to remain mindful of how local employers might be impacted. In some cases, hospitals were asked to agree to significant pricing discounts, resulting in tension between the affected parties. Physicians were also asked for pricing concessions to add another layer of complexity to the issue.

Back then, most physicians were in private practices, separate from the hospital. Yet, in communities like Gallatin, where there was only one hospital, the local physicians (generally) followed the hospital's lead. In theory, having the hospital and local physicians in the same insurance networks was in everyone's best interests. However, since the hospital had no authority to negotiate contracts on behalf of private-practice physicians, it was no surprise that some physicians elected to do their own thing.

I remember the reaction to the introduction of the first PPO network in the region. Not only did tensions escalate between the hospital, insurance companies, and local employers, but similar tensions developed between the hospital and local physicians. It was an uneasy feeling.

UNANTICIPATED OPPORTUNITY

Aside from the valuable experiences gained within the hospital and the meaningful relationships built in the community, I also seized the opportunity to expand my network of professional colleagues. As the CEO of a stand-alone community hospital, there were times when I felt that I was on an island by myself. I was eager to develop relationships with other CEOs experiencing similar challenges.

Nashville was only thirty-five miles away, making connecting with other healthcare professionals and elected officials easy. Since the Tennessee Hospital Association (THA) was based in Nashville, I prioritized getting involved with THA to establish a strong professional network and to help better understand the issues affecting healthcare across the state. Since Nashville is Tennessee's state capital, I also leveraged my involvement with THA to establish relationships with key governmental leaders.

As a bonus, Nashville was, and still is, considered a hotbed for healthcare entrepreneurial activity. Most notably, Hospital Corporation of America (HCA) was founded in Nashville and claims Nashville as its home. Hundreds of other healthcare companies are also based in Nashville, many of which were spinoffs from HCA. Living near Nashville allowed me to develop peer professional relationships with an impressive list of healthcare leaders and entrepreneurs.

My involvement with THA had another attractive tangential benefit I didn't fully anticipate. Once I started participating in THA activities, I became well known within hospital circles, and my name was often mentioned when CEO positions at other hospitals became open. I wasn't necessarily looking to leave Gallatin, so I didn't actively follow up on most of those opportunities. But one job opportunity caught my attention, and I couldn't entirely dismiss it from my mind.

One day, I received a phone call from the chairman of the board search committee of Memorial Hospital in Clarksville, Tennessee. The opportunity would represent a logical, professional progression, moving to a larger hospital in a larger community with more diverse medical programs and services. Like five years earlier, when I accepted the position in Gallatin, if I were to be selected, I would be following a long-tenured CEO who had announced his retirement. I was flattered just to be considered.

After a series of meetings, interviews, and trips to Clarksville, I was offered the position. But the decision to leave Gallatin wasn't an easy one. I had developed a strong connection with everyone associated with the hospital. My wife and I had cultivated many close friendships and relationships. I have a warm spot in my heart for the Gallatin community that remains to this day. But I had to weigh the professional opportunity with what was best for my family. Through mixed emotions of tears and excitement, I accepted the offer and submitted my resignation.

FOLLOWING A LEGEND

The year was 1989. Clarksville Memorial had just completed a major facility expansion project, adding a new wing and newly renovated spaces for several ancillary departments. New physicians had been recruited to the community, and plans were underway to initiate several new programs and services.

The city was growing and had a solid economic base, driven primarily by a core business community, Austin Peay State University, and Fort Campbell army base. All the critical ingredients for success seemed to be in place. I went into the job feeling excited and confident about the future.

There was the typical honeymoon period. My wife and I were welcomed into the community with open arms. Almost immediately, we made new friends and developed strong relationships. Likewise, I was welcomed by the staff at the hospital and the medical community. Granted, everyone wanted to share their thoughts and suggestions of things that needed attention, and I valued their input.

I did a lot of listening and relationship building. I didn't question the sincerity of those who offered opinions, but I also knew that each of them had vested interests. The more I listened, the more evident it was that those vested interests were not always aligned. I sensed that I would need to proceed with caution.

The implementation of PPS in Gallatin posed my first significant challenge. When I arrived in Clarksville, it was the evolution of managed care. I had experienced a small dose of managed care in Gallatin, with the emergence of HMOs and PPOs and contentious negotiations with insurance companies.

Once I settled in Clarksville, managed care matured even more. Like in Gallatin, Clarksville Memorial was the only hospital in the community. The difference, however, was that the medical staff was more extensive and more diverse. It was obvious that achieving 100 percent alignment between the hospital and all physicians would be impossible. As a result, I knew the honeymoon period would not last very long.

Another aspect of the honeymoon period was something I anticipated, but not to the extent that it played out. I had learned many important lessons in Gallatin by following a twenty-five-year-tenured CEO, so I thought I was prepared to do so again.

However, in Clarksville, the challenges were even more pronounced. The CEO I followed had been there for over twenty-eight years. There were essentially the same groups of people I had encountered in Gallatin ... the 25 percent who resisted change and the 25 percent who were frustrated when change didn't happen fast enough. Then there was the other 50 percent in the middle.

The biggest difference was the deep-seated loyalists to my successor. Several key staff members, including senior executives and managers, had worked with the previous CEO for decades. It was hard for them to accept a new and different leadership style. They were solidly entrenched in the change-resistant 25 percent. Two of them had been candidates for the CEO position, which posed an understandably awkward situation for me. Also, and not too uncommon in sole community hospitals, there were relatives and close friends of the former CEO working at the hospital.

COMPASSIONATE LEADERSHIP

While I didn't sense any overt criticism or resentment, there was always a lingering cloud of concern. I inherited several long-standing traditions, some of which I just learned to accept, and consciously decided to test the waters before tinkering with those traditions. When I reflect on how my experience helped prepare me for this new landscape, the 25-50-25 rule stands out as helping me fully understand and empathize with the people I was now leading. It's human nature when facing change.

CHAPTER 6

THE WILD, WILD WEST

There were days when I felt like Rocky Balboa in his first fight against Clubber Lang. The issues were coming fast and furious from all directions … right jabs, left hooks, and combination punches. I would seize any opportunity to collect my thoughts, shake off the cobwebs, and regain my composure. But the hits kept coming, faster and more furious than before.

CRUCIBLE #3:

CLINTON HEALTHCARE PLAN OF 1993

The Clinton healthcare plan of 1993 was a healthcare reform package proposed by the administration of President Bill Clinton. After taking office in 1992, Clinton moved forward with his health reform initiative by creating two independent entities to focus on healthcare reform: the Task Force on National Health Care Reform and the White House Health Care Interdepartmental Working Group. The cabinet-level Task Force was chaired by First Lady Hillary Rodham Clinton, to make recommendations to reform the US healthcare system. The primary intent of the Clinton plan was to provide universal healthcare coverage for all Americans.[16]

The concept of managed care continued to evolve. With it came a growing concern and uncertainty about the future of the US healthcare system. Healthcare costs continued to grow at an unacceptable rate despite the efforts of the federal government and the private sector. In 1992, President Bill Clinton took the oath of office and promised to deliver on a campaign promise to reform the healthcare system.

As is true with most controversial legislative efforts, the Health Security Act became a very contentious political issue. Not to dwell on the various behind-the-scenes posturing, suffice it to say that President Clinton's attempt at healthcare reform was unsuccessful. By late summer 1994, the Health Security Act was declared dead.

However, that is not to say that the attempt at healthcare reform had no impact on the healthcare system. Even though the efforts to legislate healthcare reform may have failed, the private sector embraced managed care principles. It was almost as if the governmental attempt at reform had been a catalyst for change. It fueled significant activity in the private sector, resulting in what some would characterize as chaos.

---

16   Theda Skocpol, "The Rise and Resounding Demise of the Clinton Plan," *Health Affairs* 14, no. 1 (spring 1995), doi: https://doi.org/10.1377/hlthaff.14.1.66.

CRUCIBLE #4:

TENNCARE

TennCare is the state Medicaid program in Tennessee. TennCare was established in 1994 under a federal waiver that authorized deviations from the standard Medicaid rules. It was the first state Medicaid program to enroll all Medicaid recipients in managed care. When first implemented, it also offered health insurance to other residents who did not have other insurance. Over time, the non-Medicaid component of the program was significantly reduced. Today, TennCare offers a large variety of programs to serve the citizens of Tennessee better.[17]

The concept of healthcare reform didn't stop at the federal level. In Tennessee, there was growing concern over the cost and structure of the state's Medicaid program. This garnered attention from the state legislature in the early 1990s and became a high priority for Governor Ned McWherter.[18]

The two most significant concerns about Medicaid centered around the program's growing impact on the state budget and access to affordable healthcare for the state's citizens. To address the cost issue, the traditional fee-for-service payment methodology was proposed to be eliminated and replaced with a managed care model administered by private-sector managed care organizations.

---

17 Wikipedia, "TennCare," accessed July 29, 2024, https://en.wikipedia.org/wiki/TennCare.

18 James Blumstein and Frank Sloan, "Health Care Reform through Medicaid Managed Care: Tennessee (TennCare) as a Case Study and a Paradigm," *Vanderbilt Law Review* 53, no. 1, https://scholarship.law.vanderbilt.edu/vlr/vol53/iss1/3/.

Implementing managed care principles was believed to improve utilization and cover additional people. The uninsured population could be added to the Medicaid rolls without increasing the state's budget to support the program.

In 1994, a revamped Medicaid program, TennCare, was implemented after qualifying for a federal waiver to change the payment methodology. Overnight, enrollees grew from around one million to one and a half million by expanding coverage to other eligible citizens.

Governor McWherter left office in 1995 with TennCare as one of his most notable lasting legacies. He received accolades from other parts of the country because of his innovation in expanding the Medicaid program and minimizing the impact on the state budget.

But what about healthcare providers? Essentially, much of the financial burden to make the program work fell on the backs of hospitals, physicians, and other healthcare professionals. From my perspective, it was just another challenge to add to a fast-growing list.

Suddenly, working in healthcare was like the Wild, Wild West. Everyone began jockeying for positions—hospitals and health systems (nonprofit and for-profit), physicians and physician groups, insurance companies, major employers, and managed care organizations. With every action, there was an equal and opposite reaction.

Clarksville's proximity to Nashville (just forty-five miles away) meant that Clarksville was on everyone's radar. Virtually every hospital system in Nashville started courting us as they built their referral networks. There were relatively few overtures to acquire our hospital, but we were certainly getting a lot of attention. It was as if we were the prettiest girls at the dance, and everyone wanted the opportunity to dance with us.

CRUCIBLE #5:

BALANCED BUDGET ACT OF 1997

The Balanced Budget Act was enacted in 1997 by the US Congress as an omnibus legislative package designed to balance the federal budget by 2002. Medicare payments to healthcare providers were cut by $112 billion, a significant portion of which targeted hospitals.[19]

In 1997, Congress enacted the Balanced Budget Act to help balance the federal budget. Reimbursement to hospitals took another hit. This law didn't generate as much attention as PPS, but its effect on hospitals was equally impactful. It added another layer of pressure on hospitals' financial viability, but its impact sometimes gets overlooked. Nevertheless, it was significant.

THE LOCAL MEDICAL COMMUNITY

Locally, there were some other interesting dynamics and developments. A freestanding ambulatory surgery center was built in the community, with several local physicians as investors. Additionally, a growing number of physician practices began providing ancillary services, such as lab and imaging, as an extension of their practices.

I fully understood that such developments were consistent with healthcare trends across the country and that those trends would likely continue to grow as more services shifted to an outpatient setting. However, since much of the hospital's revenue stream depended on

---

19   Congressional Budget Office, "CBO Memorandum," December 1997, accessed July 29, 2024, https://www.cbo.gov/sites/default/files/105th-congress-1997-1998/reports/bba-97.pdf.

those services, it certainly financially impacted the hospital. It was my responsibility to ensure that the hospital operated in a financially prudent manner, and that responsibility just got more difficult.

Much of the healthcare literature of the day was pessimistic about the future of doctor-hospital relationships. Some feared that the hospital's biggest competitor in the future would be its medical staff. There would likely be financial incentives for physicians to perform imaging studies and ancillary testing procedures in their private offices rather than in the hospital. This would be a significant development and loss of revenue, and hospitals would need to adjust. That prediction was coming true right before my eyes.

Despite some of these troubling trends, we initiated discussions with our physicians about a unified effort to deal with managed care. Hospitals in other regions of the country had created legal structures known as physician-hospital organizations (PHOs) to negotiate managed care contracts for both the hospital and physicians. The PHO was seen as one contracting model that would avoid antitrust concerns.

The concept was a good one in theory and indeed appeared to be a logical and reasonable option. But what seems logical and sensible in theory doesn't always work as envisioned. In our case, several other developments added more layers of complexity.

Independent of the hospital's attempts to develop a community-wide strategy, some physicians began to formulate their own strategy. Perhaps the most game-changing example was when several physicians formed a multispecialty group that included almost half of the hospital's medical staff. The impetus behind that group formation was to achieve collective strength in managed care contract negotiations.

Then, within a few months, and in somewhat of a response to the multispecialty group, another group of physicians formed an independent physician association (IPA). While the IPA structure was different from the multispecialty group model, the intent was similar. Physicians aligning together under a common organizational structure would provide more strength in negotiating reimbursement rates with insurance companies and managed care organizations, rather than those same physicians negotiating individually. A third group was formed, primarily composed of hospital-based specialties.

Whew!

It was certainly very different from the old days when a cohesive medical staff comprised all physicians in the community. As may be obvious, the objectives of each group and their envisioned relationship with the hospital were vastly different. Animosities developed between former colleagues, and strained relationships grew. My job focus shifted from working with one unified medical staff to interacting with three separate groups while protecting the hospital's interests. My list of challenges just got a whole lot more difficult.

THE VALUE OF COMMUNITY SERVICE

I tried not to dwell on the negative. By nature, I consider myself more of an optimist. To help compensate for the growing list of challenges, I made time to remain active and involved with THA and other healthcare organizations. I was elected to the THA board of directors and chairman of one of its subsidiaries. I valued those opportunities to serve healthcare and stay abreast of new developments.

I have always felt that the CEO of a community hospital should support the local community and participate in community activities. Given the time commitment, I was somewhat selective about which organizations I chose to be involved with. I also felt that it was essential to participate in organizations whose values aligned with my values. In addition to being a member of the Clarksville Rotary Club and an active member of our church, I also became active in the Clarksville Chamber of Commerce. I was elected chairman of the chamber board and the economic development committee. I also served as campaign chair for the annual United Way campaign.

There is a sense of gratification that comes with community service. In retrospect, those opportunities also helped me retain a healthy work-life balance. Participating in community activities provided a needed respite from the daily grind at the hospital. It also served to fuel my desire to do something positive and meaningful for the community. As a result, I sensed that my batteries were recharged, allowing me to be more productive at work and more attentive to my family's needs.

NOW IT GETS COMPLICATED

The job description of any hospital CEO includes working closely with the board to review and update the hospital's strategic plan. In the mid-1990s, it was obvious that healthcare was changing rapidly, and we needed to have a clear vision of our future direction.

Upon my recommendation, the board engaged an outside consultant to assist with this critical initiative. We spent countless hours analyzing data and evaluating every aspect of the organization. We conducted an environmental assessment and identified our strengths, weaknesses, opportunities, and threats.

As part of the process, the consultant required all board and executive team members to read a recently published book, *Built to Last* by Collins and Porras.[20] While not explicitly focused on healthcare, this book encouraged us to envision what we could accomplish if

---

20   James C. Collins and Jerry I. Porras, *Built to Last* (Harper Business, 1994).

we allowed ourselves to dream big. The "Big Hairy Audacious Goals"[21] described in the book became our rallying cry to help us broaden our vision.

As an outgrowth of that planning process, my most controversial and time-consuming project was yet to come. Clarksville Memorial Hospital opened its doors in 1954 as a Hospital District, jointly created by the city and county governments. As such, it was a public (governmental) hospital, subject to governmental guidelines and restrictions. This was identified as a potential weakness, leading us to reevaluate the hospital's legal structure.

As a governmental entity, there was a growing concern about the flexibility needed in the ever-changing healthcare environment. For example, could the hospital joint-venture with other parties, could the hospital operate across state lines, and could the hospital employ physicians? Were there other activities that would be prohibited as a governmental entity that might put the hospital at a competitive disadvantage?

After multiple strategic planning meetings and discussions, the board voted to retain the services of a law firm specializing in corporate restructuring. This decision was made because of the unique intricacies of healthcare and because the process would involve interacting with multiple governmental entities at city, county, and state levels. Federal laws and Medicare regulations also need to be considered. No local or regional law firms had such specialized expertise; therefore, a nationally recognized law firm with experience in this area was selected to guide the process.

Then, the real work began. We reviewed the charter that created the Hospital District, and then determined what steps would be required to change it. Since the city and county governments had

---

21   Ibid.

created the original Hospital District, any changes had to be approved by both entities.

A resolution was drafted by our legal counsel and reviewed by the respective city and county attorneys, then finalized for approval by the city council and the county commission. Any time the wording of the resolution was changed by either party, it had to go back to the other party for ratification. It took four votes by the city council and four votes by the county commission before it was finally approved. Then it had to go to the state of Tennessee for final approval, which was granted with no noted concerns. The state's approval was confirmation that our hard work and collective efforts had paid off. It was a gratifying sense of accomplishment.

Another aspect of the process was the creation of a new private, not-for-profit corporation to assume hospital operations. Clarksville Memorial Hospital became Clarksville Regional Health System. Two years later, to create a new brand, the name was changed to Gateway Health System. All board members were required to resign from the former board, and because the board of the new corporation was smaller in size, not all former board members were appointed to the new board. That became a somewhat sensitive issue, but ultimately, it worked out.

I wish I had kept a tally of the total hours I spent on this project. Suffice it to say it consumed most of my time for about a year and a half. And that doesn't even reflect the many questions thrown at me during the process. I did my best to keep the hospital employees and medical staff informed every step of the way. However, some remained skeptical.

The hardest questions came at public meetings, in front of the city council and county commission. The press was also present because they were public meetings, which usually generated interesting headlines in the local newspaper the following morning. There were occasions when I felt like I was not just defending the rationale behind the proposed change but also defending my integrity. This was an era when, in many communities across the land, the local press became adversarial to the community leadership. Investigative teams fanned out and looked for things that could be questioned.

I learned that local politics can be brutal, and I was an easy target. I fully understood that the entire process represented significant change, which is problematic. However, I also knew that the change was important for the future viability of the hospital.

The most contentious issues revolved around the financial aspects of the restructuring. Some local officials were skeptical that money was being funneled under the table and that some individuals might benefit financially. Because of my position and the fact that I was the hospital spokesman at most public meetings, much of that skepticism was directed at me. I admit that it hurt my feelings to have my integrity questioned, but I had to maintain a sense of professionalism throughout the process. As much as anything, local governmental leaders, including city and county officials, wanted to be assured that the ownership and control of the hospital remained local. The hospital was viewed as a valuable community asset that had to be preserved.

A commonly used phrase when things seem to be spinning out of control is "Are we having fun yet?" Well, that is how I felt as the issues continued evolving. My list of challenges grew longer by the day: TennCare, managed care, regional healthcare networks, strained physician relationships, growing competition, corporate restructuring, and skepticism among the news media. Every issue was important, and every issue required my undivided attention.

THE HITS KEPT COMING

Moviegoers will recall that Rocky had gained tremendous popularity and was the reigning heavyweight champion of the world. But an up-and-coming boxer, Clubber Lang, had risen to prominence and was ready to challenge Rocky for the title. Rocky starts the fight by landing several punches. Lang seemed unfazed and fought back with a series of fast and furious blows, ultimately knocking Rocky out in the second round.

> *There were days when I felt like Rocky Balboa in his first fight against Clubber Lang. The issues were coming fast and furious from all directions ... right jabs, left hooks, and combination punches. I would seize any opportunity to collect my thoughts, shake off the cobwebs, and regain my composure. But the hits kept coming, faster and more furious than before.*

My last two years in Clarksville were, without a doubt, the most challenging of my professional career. Healthcare had experienced rapid changes. Reimbursement incentives from third-party payers and managed care contracts often pitted hospitals and physicians against each other, and sometimes physician groups against each other.

The fragmentation within the medical community made it difficult, if not impossible, to keep everyone working in alignment. Following the successful corporate restructuring, the hospital board had gained a renewed sense of energy and was ready to assert its newly realized independence. Yet the political fallout and alienation that had resulted from separating from city and county government led to some bitter feelings on the part of governmental leaders.

I had multiple constituencies I was trying to please, each with different priorities and expectations. When I drove to work each morning, I didn't know who would be mad at me that day, but I knew someone would.

By the time I arrived at the office, I was already starting to tense up. I rarely ate breakfast, knowing that it would only lead to indigestion. As an alternative, I chose to rely on several cups of black coffee to keep me going. The caffeine seemed to work, but that was only temporary. The headaches set in by lunchtime, and an empty stomach didn't help. I tried to relax long enough to eat a healthy meal but rarely had much appetite. Emotionally, I sensed that I was uptight more than usual, and my self-confidence slowly eroded.

To compensate, I started working long hours in a futile attempt to stay on top of every important issue. I was working six, sometimes seven days a week, yet it felt like I was always playing catch-up. I would leave home early each morning and stay at work until late. It was not uncommon for me to go several days without seeing my kids awake. They were asleep when I left to go to work and safely back in bed when I returned home. I started missing some of their events … soccer games, dance recitals, and church programs. It greatly burdened my wife to keep our family unit functioning. I can't thank her enough for managing through those difficult times.

My health began to suffer, both mentally and physically. I felt significant pressure, yet I kept much of it to myself. I wasn't comfortable confiding in others, not knowing how they might react. I even kept some things from my wife, something I now regret. I'm not a clinician, so I can't say that I was experiencing clinical depression. But I knew that I was frequently down in the dumps and had a severe case of the blues.

THE LAST TRAIN TO CLARKSVILLE

I've always heard that perceptions vary from person to person, but everyone's perception is real. Changing one's perception of a person or an issue can be difficult, if not impossible. After I had been in my position in Clarksville for a few years, I experienced something that illustrates how greatly perceptions can differ.

One morning, I was sitting at my desk when a long-tenured, well-respected physician knocked on my door and asked if I had a few minutes to talk. I wasn't expecting him, but I certainly made the time. My first reaction was to brace myself for another complaint, which is usually the case when a physician shows up unannounced. But I was pleasantly surprised. He wanted to compliment me on the positive changes I had made at the hospital. He said that my appointment as CEO had been "refreshing" and that he was amazed at all I had accomplished in such a short time.

He said I was very bright and skilled at handling contentious issues with professionalism and diplomacy. He acknowledged that physicians' personalities can be difficult, but I dealt with them with patience, poise, and confidence. I was caught off guard by his compliments but thanked him, nevertheless.

That made my day. Rarely did I receive such spur-of-the-moment compliments. I floated on air for the next few hours and had an extra pep in my step. After all I had been through for the past few years, I felt I had arrived.

The very next day, another physician knocked on my door and wanted to talk. I thought I must be on a roll, and another round of compliments was forthcoming, but that was not the case. This physician had a very different perception of my performance. In so many words, he unloaded on me with both barrels.

He started by voicing all his frustrations with the hospital, some of which predated me. These included outdated equipment, run-down facilities, incompetent staff, and poor management. He even took a few shots at the hospital's board of directors. He said that he had been hopeful that I would bring a fresh view and would have resolved all his issues by now.

I can almost quote verbatim his most damning comment, *You have been here for almost five years and have accomplished virtually nothing. Isn't it time you get off your a** and do something?*

Two very different perceptions and two very different conversations were delivered just twenty-four hours apart. Suddenly, I was no longer on cloud nine, and the pep in my step was long gone. I wanted to go off somewhere by myself and sulk.

CLOUDED JUDGMENT

I wish I had pulled that old book, *Judgment in Administration*, off the shelf and reread it because I knew I was not exercising very good judgment. I was making some ill-advised decisions, which I now attribute to stress. I was trying too hard to please everyone, and by doing so, rarely pleased anyone.

But when a half-dozen constituents were tugging at me from different directions, sometimes my sense of reason became clouded. I needed a break but didn't know how to make it happen. I had gone almost two years without taking a real vacation, other than a few days here and there. I realize now how unhealthy that can be.

I wasn't pleased with my performance, and I sensed that the medical staff and hospital board weren't either. There was too much turmoil, some of which was out of my control, some of which was of my own doing. I sensed that something had to give. In my introspective way, I knew that the hospital deserved better leadership. I was exhausted, and I needed some relief. If nothing else, my family needed me, and I needed them.

So, after a great deal of thought and prayer, then a lot more thought and prayer, I resigned.

Decisions such as this are never easy. Throughout my lifetime, I have prided myself on not being a quitter. But this was different. Multiple considerations came into play, not the least of which was the well-being of the hospital, my family, and me. My faith in God was challenged like never before, but ultimately, the experience made my faith even stronger. There was a sense of peace and affirmation that could only come from hours of prayer and divine guidance.

COMPASSIONATE LEADERSHIP

These were tough days, and I remember one evening driving away from the hospital and turning on the local country music station. I found myself listening to country star Kenny Rogers sing "The Gambler." His words were simple but meaningful. I sensed that it was time for me to fold my hand and walk away.

CHAPTER 7

ONE DOOR CLOSES, ANOTHER OPENS

> *Every arrow in my leadership quiver had been exhausted.*

t first, there was relief and a sense of freedom. The issues that had consumed most of my waking moments for two years could finally be set aside. I could relax, take a deep breath, and enjoy my family again. It was as if a giant pressure valve had been inserted into my body, and all that pent-up pressure had been relieved.

But the future suddenly became cloudier, and my patience was tested. Alexander Graham Bell once said:

When one door closes, another door opens; but we often look so long and so regretfully upon the closed door that we do not see the ones which open for us. [22]

---

22 Rose Leadem, "12 Inspiring Quotes from the Inventor of the Telephone, Alexander Graham Bell," *Entrepeneur*, March 10, 2017, accessed February 14, 2024, https://www. entrepreneur.com/leadership/12-inspiring-quotes-from-the-inventor-of-the-telephone/290418.

While I wasn't sure how, when, or where, I had to rely on my faith that another door would open. Ironically, a few doors had already cracked open, which I didn't fully appreciate at the time. My professional network kicked into high gear behind the scenes, and I began getting calls from friends and colleagues, some of whom I had considered working for or with at different times.

But I didn't want to act too quickly without giving all my options adequate thought, consideration, and prayer. I needed time to reflect, decompress, and evaluate. In essence, I wanted to take the same systematic approach in making an important decision as I had done all those years in my professional life.

It meant reevaluating my career goals, so I conducted a 360-degree self-assessment. I listed my self-identified strengths and weaknesses. I was hard on myself and made a list of probing questions as part of the process. Was I cut out for this type of work? Did I have the skills necessary to be successful in today's healthcare environment? Should I consider a career outside of healthcare? I had lots of questions but very few answers.

Despite my efforts to avoid doing so, I spent time (maybe too much time, according to Alexander Graham Bell) reflecting on the past two years. My self-critique probably focused too much on what I hadn't done rather than what I needed to do. What could I have done differently? What did I overlook that I should have seen? Where did I go wrong? On a personal basis, I struggled with how my relationships with other people had been affected. Who had I offended? Who did I let down? Had I been unfair in my dealings?

My propensity to play the twenty-twenty-hindsight game made it difficult to focus on the future, but I suppose that is human nature.

Reflecting on those last two turbulent years in Clarksville,
I can now see that every arrow in my leadership quiver had
been exhausted.

As noted earlier, the issues were complex, and the number of people simultaneously pulling my chain grew by the day. There were days when I had difficulty prioritizing what needed to be done.

I was reminded of a saying I read in the executive restroom adjacent to my boss's office during my early years at Fort Sanders. On those occasions when he was out of the office, I used to sneak into his private restroom rather than take the long walk down the hallway to the public men's room. Posted on the inside of the door was a nicely framed plaque that read:

When you are up to your neck in alligators, it's hard
to remember that your initial objective was to drain the
swamp.[23]

I have seen various versions of that quote over the years (some with a bit more colorful language); however, the meaning is clear. And if there is any consolation, I somehow felt comforted that others, like my mentor, had encountered similar challenges. I wasn't alone.

---

23   Lillee Gelinas, "Alligators, Swamps, and Medication Safety," *American Nurse*, January 10, 2023, accessed February 13, 2024, https://www.myamericannurse.com/alligators-swamps-and-medication-safety/#:~:text=An%20old%20adage%20says%2C%20%E2%80%9CWhen,your%20primary%20purpose%20while%20coping, January 20, 2023.

CAREER TURBULENCE IS NORMAL

One of the doors that opened for me took me down a somewhat unconventional path. It was an opportunity still connected to healthcare, but my new role was as a consultant rather than traditional hospital management.

A longtime professional associate of mine was the founder and principal of a healthcare information technology consulting firm in Nashville. He wanted to expand his group's offerings to hospitals and invited me to be part of that vision. My background in hospital operations and extensive professional network could benefit the company as new products and services were developed. His invitation was an answer to my prayer, and I sincerely appreciated the opportunity.

It was an exciting time and served to reenergize and refocus my professional aspirations. I thought that healthcare was changing rapidly, but I hadn't seen anything like the fast-paced changes occurring in the world of technology. E-commerce was beginning to reshape business in the US, and the dot-com movement was gaining steam. Our primary customers were hospitals struggling to keep up with technological innovations and needed additional expertise to help determine their future direction. In some cases, hospitals were interested in outsourcing options to relieve the burden of significant financial investments in hardware, software, and associated operational costs.

Expanding and enhancing that outsourcing model was seen as a timely and potentially lucrative business opportunity for the consulting firm. Admittedly, information technology was not my strongest suit, so I found myself "drinking from a fire hose," but I enjoyed the experience.

But an underlying sense of uneasiness kept nagging at me. After a few months, the thrill of the ride began to wane. Yes, I shared some of my operational expertise, and my professional network helped to open a few doors, but I felt like a fish out of water. Without the technical knowledge and expertise, my role was somewhat limited. The technology industry continued to evolve at a rapid pace.

The dot-com bubble started to deflate, and with it came a ripple effect on other sectors of the technology world. Venture capitalists pulled back on planned investments, and there was a general pause in the action. The firm I was associated with was also faced with modifying strategic decisions, and as a result, some of their plans had to be put on hold. At about the same time, that uncomfortable nagging feeling kept churning, and oddly enough, I found myself missing the hustle and bustle of the hospital.

That's when my faith was tested even further. However, that old Alexander Graham Bell adage somehow came true again. I received a phone call from the president and CEO of the Baptist Health System of East Tennessee in Knoxville. One of the senior executives at Baptist had recently resigned to take another opportunity, and the executive vice president position was open. I was asked if I would be interested in returning to Knoxville and joining the Baptist Health System.

Knoxville had been my home for the first seven and a half years of my professional career. It was a city I was very familiar with. Furthermore, it was home to my wife and the town where we had met and were married. Aside from the professional opportunity, returning to Knoxville was appealing for several reasons.

As might be expected, the healthcare landscape in Knoxville had changed significantly in the seventeen and a half years since I had left. Four regional hospital systems evolved through a series of mergers and acquisitions during that time. Ironically, one of Baptist's main competitors, Covenant Health, included Fort Sanders Regional Medical

Center, where my professional career began. That would be somewhat awkward, but it didn't deter my interest in returning to Knoxville.

Other, more compelling reasons merited serious consideration. First, the Baptist Health System's faith-based mission aligned perfectly with my values. Second, Baptist had been recognized as one of the top one hundred hospitals in the US and had recently received approval to build a new satellite hospital in a growing part of the service area. Third, Knoxville was poised for continued growth and was considered one of the most attractive cities to raise a family.

When offered the position, I felt a peace I hadn't felt in years. After my brief tenure as a consultant, I concluded that I was probably better suited for a more conventional hospital role. After all, healthcare administration was more closely aligned with my education, training, and experience.

As I prepared to move my family back to Knoxville in 2001, I couldn't have been more excited. Everything about the opportunity felt right. But that didn't mean that things would get any easier. The ever-changing healthcare landscape and the unique challenges of transitioning to a new organizational culture posed some steep hills. I quickly learned to buckle my seatbelt and prepare for a bumpy road ahead.

COMPASSIONATE LEADERSHIP

As I said, by now, I was aware of the giant pressure valve that healthcare had inserted into my body, and it seemed that all that pent-up pressure had been relieved. Nothing could stress me now. I had come through the gauntlet and was ready for a refreshing change. One of the things that troubled me most during the height of that storm was my limited ability to change things, to make things better for my people.

Make a note of that. It's not a good sign when your compassionate leadership runs out of playing field. You may also miss the memo saying that there is no guarantee that the new playing field will accommodate your carefully composed compassionate leadership philosophy.

PART TWO

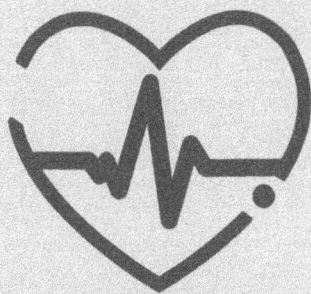

CHAPTER 8

DIVERSE PERSPECTIVES

> *Most healthcare executives will admit that they suffered many sleepless nights.*

n one of the most memorable scenes in the movie *Rocky III*, a reporter asks Clubber Lang, "What is your prediction for the fight?" He responds with a straightforward, intentionally threatening, one-word answer ... "*Pain.*"

That single word sets the stage for the main event yet to come, and his serious, eye-piercing facial expression adds an extra degree of emphasis, keeping the audience on the edge of their seats.

Granted, the fight between Rocky Balboa and Clubber Lang is fictitious. But real-life prizefighters will admit they endure tremendous pain during a typical boxing match, a pain to which few of us can relate.

On average, delivering a punch takes about six-hundredths of a second. Bloody noses, cuts above the eyes, busted lips, broken bones, and concussions can be commonplace. Yet even though fighters experience significant pain, their training prepares them to tolerate it and focus on the task at hand. The consequences of the pain would be dealt with later.

Leaders deal with different types of stress and pain. They may not have bloodied noses and broken bones, but the emotional toll is real. The relentless frequency of challenging issues can have the same effect on one's well-being as if a professional boxer were delivering split-second punches. My personal experiences certainly bear this out. There were many times during my career when I felt that I had survived twelve to fifteen rounds with Clubber Lang.

However, rather than relying on my experiences alone, I sense that the perspectives of others might be more meaningful and would better illustrate the issues that healthcare leaders routinely face. So, before continuing with my story, I'd like to pause to interject some thoughts and insights from several of my most respected professional colleagues. These are individuals who are former classmates, coworkers, professional peers, and trusted friends. Most of them are now retired after very successful careers.

Collectively, these individuals have logged over five hundred years of experience as healthcare executives. I appreciate their willingness to offer their input and feel confident that their viewpoints will help to shine additional light on these complex issues.

CEOs are paid to make hard decisions. That goes with the territory. Professional organizations such as the ACHE will periodically poll their membership to get a feel for the most challenging issues that healthcare executives are dealing with.[24]

---

24 "Top Issues Confronting Hospitals," American College of Healthcare Executives, accessed October 23, 2024, https://www.ache.org/learning-center/research/about-the-field/top-issues-confronting-hospitals.

The ACHE drilled down a bit and reported that staffing shortages across the employment spectrum were a constant worry, with nursing being a top concern.

As part of the survey, a frequently asked question is "What are the top issues confronting hospitals?" Responses to this question can vary according to the crisis du jour, but generally, a few consistent themes highlight the most pressing issues.

When I asked my CEO colleagues what types of decisions were the most difficult to make, three primary themes were apparent: (1) issues that affected employees' jobs, (2) issues related to changing organizational culture, and (3) physician relationship issues.[25]

ISSUES THAT AFFECT EMPLOYEES' JOBS

When the Medicare PPS was implemented in the mid-1980s, hospitals were forced to right-size accordingly. The three-headed monster of preadmission certification, utilization review, and length-of-stay restrictions dramatically impacted the utilization of inpatient services.

Almost overnight, the number of hospital beds needed to care for Medicare patients was reduced significantly. Hospitals adjusted by closing nursing units and reducing the number of staffed beds. Consequently, staffing levels decreased because hospitals could no longer justify the number of employees previously needed during pre-PPS times. Downsizings, reductions in force, and layoffs became commonly used buzzwords nationwide. Hospitals of all shapes and sizes had to deal with this issue, and it was a very unpleasant and agonizing task.

Healthcare executives found themselves facing a very gut-wrenching dilemma. From a dollars-and-cents standpoint, downsizing was a

25   Ibid.

no-brainer. It had to be done. Other businesses had been accustomed to making routine staffing adjustments. Product production seasonality in many industries often led to manufacturing cutbacks and plant closures at certain times of the year. But healthcare was different. Besides a decrease in admissions for a few days during the Christmas holidays, the demand for hospital services was relatively constant, and the healthcare workforce was somewhat stable.

Most healthcare executives were unfamiliar with the thought of laying off staff. In addition, hospitals, by their very nature, have a caring culture. Hospital workers care for patients, but they also care for each other. This is true at virtually every level of the organization, whether clinical, support, or administrative. The attitude of caring is pervasive throughout most healthcare organizations. These people are called upon to offer a full commitment to the hospital, no matter the challenge. How do you say to them, "Your job is gone"?

So, the decision to eliminate jobs was inherently difficult. People's livelihoods, including those of their immediate and extended families, were affected. Most healthcare executives will admit that they suffered many sleepless nights, knowing that pending layoffs were imminent.

> *Most healthcare executives will admit that they suffered many sleepless nights.*

Healthcare executives also had to be mindful of how sensitive employee-relations issues could lead to union-organizing activity. Collective bargaining in hospitals began to gain steam during the 1970s, which created another element of concern any time decisions were made that affected a hospital's workforce. Among issues such as unfair management practices, poor working conditions, and pay disparities, a reduction in force, if not handled correctly, could likely open the door to union activity.

ISSUES RELATED TO CHANGING ORGANIZATIONAL CULTURE

Similarly, the challenges of changing organizational culture are equally tricky. Some would argue that an organization's culture is already established and that new leaders should adjust accordingly. Others would suggest that change is necessary as the external environment changes.

One professional colleague cited the example of changing the culture and mindset of a hospital that opened as a Hill-Burton facility in the 1950s. (Hill-Burton was a bonanza for hospital construction across America.) On August 13, 1946, the Hill-Burton Act was signed into law by President Harry S. Truman. The bill, known formally as the Hospital Survey and Construction Act, was a Truman initiative that provided construction grants and loans to build hospitals where they were needed and would be sustainable.[26]

Hospitals during that era were less complex. Reimbursement was important, but it was mainly a function of the daily room rate and "chargemaster." The focus on cost control and utilization was an afterthought. Competition among hospitals and other healthcare providers was moderate, so the attention to customer service and patient satisfaction was minimal.

All of that changed as the healthcare environment evolved. PPS forced hospitals to be concerned with cost control and prudent utilization of healthcare services. Then, as managed care evolved, so did

---

26 "Hill-Burton Act," Perspectives of Change, accessed October 25, 2024, https://perspectivesofchange.hms.harvard.edu/node/23#:~:text=On%20August%2013%2C%201946%2C%20the,needed%20and%20would%20be%20sustainable.

competition between healthcare providers. Consumers of healthcare services (patients and insurance plans) began to emphasize quality, cost, and service. Hence, hospitals had to up their game to compete.

This was an entirely different mindset for many hospital workers. There was a renewed focus on customer service and the importance of developing customer loyalty by delivering high-quality, cost-effective services. In some cases, it required a total cultural overhaul led by executive management.

This change revolution in hospitals has often been compared to changing the course of a battleship. It takes time and effort, and it doesn't just happen quickly. The qualities expected of healthcare leaders include a relentless work ethic, a change-agent mindset, and unwavering determination. Leaders can expect resistance and pushback from employees, physicians, and key stakeholders. And in most cases, the hospital CEO is the most visible and vulnerable target.

Change doesn't come easy, but sometimes changes are necessary for the organization to survive. Healthcare is an ever-changing environment, and leading change is one of the most important qualities of a successful leader.

As in most professions, healthcare executives continue to learn lessons along the way. Most executives begin their careers after going through a rigorous education process, at the very least having earned a master's degree in a related discipline. The academic process is vital in establishing a foundation upon which real-world experiences can be built. Because of the dynamic and ever-changing healthcare environment, real-world experiences and lessons learned become extremely important to leadership success.

My network of professional colleagues unanimously agrees with this premise. One colleague went so far as to say that traditional management principles of the past are no longer relevant in today's environment. Most skills needed by twenty-first-century leaders are learned in the field, not in the classroom. Servant leadership is necessary today much more than the old-school autocratic leadership.

Leaders are essentially coaches and must develop the skills necessary to build successful teams. Leaders who rely on outdated management philosophies should notice that the world around them has changed. Today's leaders need to be nimble and make changes quickly and decisively. The time-consuming decision-making processes of the past are no longer relevant.

PHYSICIAN RELATIONSHIP ISSUES

A third category of difficult decisions unanimously mentioned by my colleagues includes issues involving physicians. Some suggest that physician relations are the riskiest and potentially most volatile aspect of any hospital CEO's job. The relationships between hospitals and physicians are somewhat unique, although those relationships continue to evolve.

Hospitals and doctors enjoyed a necessary but sometimes contentious, symbiotic relationship during my hospital career. Patients were admitted and discharged upon the physician's order. The hospital staff performed diagnostic testing and procedures per the physician's order. Physicians performed surgical procedures. Hospitals needed physicians, and physicians needed hospitals.

The hospital-physician relationship was close but still at arm's length. Physicians were granted privileges to admit and treat patients in the hospital through a defined credentialing process, which required a collaborative effort between the medical staff, administration, and board of directors. Some refer to this as the three-legged stool. Mostly, physicians were not employed by the hospital but were independent practitioners who had been granted privileges to practice there.[27]

For hospital executives, the credentialing process could be a bit nerve-racking. The determination and definition of the specific privileges granted to physicians fell under the auspices of the medical staff, and the ultimate granting of privileges was the responsibility of the hospital board. However, the hospital administration often conducted much of the legwork. Most of the time, this was a routine process, yet sometimes it was far from it.

Difficult decisions arise when information raises a red flag during the credentialing process. It could be as simple as a physician requesting to perform procedures for which they aren't qualified. These could be handled objectively by closely evaluating the physician's education and training.

But there were also credentialing issues that were more problematic and sensitive … situations that involved a history of substance abuse, criminal activity, or health issues (physical or mental) that might compromise a physician's ability to practice. Sometimes, there were turf battles between specialties and competitive issues between physicians of the same specialty. While those issues are handled objectively, sometimes they can become very messy as the process unfolds. Since the hospital administration is tasked with gathering and verifying pertinent information, the hospital CEO is often where the buck stops.

Issues involving contractual relationships between hospitals and physicians can also be very stressful. Any time a financial relationship exists between a physician (or a group of physicians) and the hospital,

---

27 Disclaimer: *It should be noted that this model has changed significantly over the years. Hospitals now employ an increasing number of physicians, so the relationships are inherently different in today's healthcare environment.*

there is potential for disagreement. Each party is looking out for their best interests, which is understandable. In most cases, differences of opinion can be resolved during the negotiation process.

However, negotiations might fall through when the respective parties are miles apart, and the involved parties may choose to go their separate ways. Sometimes, the hospital CEO makes that decision; sometimes, it is made by the physicians.

Either way, the result may lead to hard feelings and the potential for additional repercussions and fallout from other physicians. Sensitive contract negotiations between hospitals and physicians have the potential to create long-standing tension and animosity within the medical community.

I suggest that young executives be fully prepared and attend classes in win-win negotiations. Win-win is a frame of mind and heart that constantly seeks mutual benefit in all human interactions. I believe that a win-win mentality is possible in healthcare, and developing these skills in the future will be essential. It means agreements or solutions are mutually beneficial and satisfying. This goes back to an empathetic ear, the art of listening and walking in another's shoes. It's dealing with your doctors as dance partners (not enemies, not competitors, not adversaries).

As an extension of that theme, another colleague noted the importance of taking the necessary time to reach a decision, but then being prepared to act quickly and decisively. Don't delay in making tough decisions. Be willing to own your decisions, admit your mistakes, and be transparent in your communication with all affected parties.

The best book I have read on this topic was written by former healthcare executives who also happened to be college football and NFL referees. *You Threw the Flag ... Now ... You Make the Call* by Ned and Dan Wilford[28] is an excellent compilation of real-life examples of challenging decisions. Whether it be in the hospital or on the football field, decision-makers must stand by their decisions.

The importance of being a good listener was also noted. Anyone who has read Stephen Covey's book *The 7 Habits of Highly Effective People* has Habit Five etched in their mind: "Seek First to Understand, Then to Be Understood."[29]

It takes patience and practice to be a good listener. Covey refers to this as "empathic listening,"[30] listening intently to what others are saying before reaching a conclusion. This helps to avoid mistakes and misdirection, especially for leaders who are new to an organization. One of my professional colleagues shared with me that this was the *single most important lesson learned* during his career.

COMPASSIONATE LEADERSHIP

Earlier in our story, I described a week during which one physician generously praised my work, quite unexpectedly, and then one day later, another physician tore me to shreds. The key word there is empathetic listening. You never know where an expected compliment can turn into an ugly personal attack. So, learning how to set your stance for walking in their shoes, recognizing the pressures that the dance partners you have must be under, and trying to have an empathetic ear with everyone can be a strategy that lifts all boats.

---

28 Ned Wilford and Dan Wilford, *You Threw the Flag ... Now ... You Make the Call* (Tapestry Press, 2022).

29 Stephen R. Covey, *The 7 Habits of Highly Effective People* (Simon and Schuster, 1989).

30 Ibid.

CHAPTER 9

THE IMPACT OF THE VELOCITY OF CHANGE IN HEALTHCARE

Herein lies the major difference between healthcare leaders and most business leaders.

have taken us on a trip down memory lane to help younger executives understand more of how healthcare evolved over the past four decades, mainly from a humanistic and financial viewpoint. All that seemed to go by at a doable pace as we lived it and adjusted our entire organization to new rules in reimbursement, competition, and human relations. There was no parachute. It was our turn to jump out of a perfectly good airplane. And totally up to us to land on our feet.

I do not need to remind everyone of the era of fast-paced technological change. But it bears bringing this part of the story forward right now because the pace of change has become phenomenal. By the early 2000s, technology had advanced such that hospitals began implementing software to create seamless systems through which financial, clinical, and statistical information could be managed. Recommendations proposed by the Leapfrog Group, described in more detail later in this chapter, added another layer of urgency. One of the fundamental initiatives of the Leapfrog Group centered around the adoption of a computerized physician order entry system for the ordering of prescription drugs administered to patients in hospitals. This was a primary area of focus because of an estimated 98,000 annual unnecessary hospital deaths, many of which were attributed to medication errors.

Few businesses have been impacted by new technology more than healthcare. We buy a new CT scanner now, and in a year, it will be obsolete. We build an electronic medical record, and we will spend the next twenty years modifying it to accommodate new demands and new diagnostic technologies. Training thousands of providers and staff to use the new medical-record system never stops.

We train our nurses well in our nursing schools, and they never stop returning for advanced degrees. Our doctors must constantly attend specialty updates to keep pace with new studies, new findings, new cures, and new demands from board certifications.

On the clinical side, virtually every aspect of healthcare has been impacted. Everything from basic instruments like thermometers and stethoscopes to large, multimillion-dollar equipment such as scanners and surgical robots. The delivery of patient care in the 2000s has almost no resemblance to how patient care was delivered in the 1960s. All of healthcare has been revolutionized and enhanced by new technology.

But it has come with a price. Hospitals have had to embrace new technology to remain competitive. It is much more than just keeping up with the Joneses. Physician recruitment, patient confidence, and the criteria to participate in insurance networks have mandated that hospitals have the latest and greatest technology. Given their size and access to capital, large medical centers and multihospital systems have, for the most part, been able to stay abreast of new clinical technology. However, it has been very challenging for small and rural hospitals, further fueling the trend of hospital consolidation through mergers and acquisitions.

In 2009, healthcare faced another key legislative mandate to enhance information technology. The Health Information Technology for Economic and Clinical Health Act was enacted to promote the adoption and meaningful use of health information technology. In simple terms, this legislation established expectations for hospitals to elevate their clinical technology capabilities to comply with HIPAA (medical-record privacy protection) and expand the use of electronic medical records.

Hospitals could face financial penalties if certain standards were not implemented. Private physician practices were also included in these mandates. Large medical centers and multihospital systems generally had the expertise and resources to meet these standards, or at least develop a timeline for implementation. However, small and rural hospitals continued to be challenged to meet the basic criteria. The financial investments needed to comply with the standards were simply too great.

Among others, two books I've read on the topic of change stand out, both of which highlight the importance of managing organizational change effectively. The first, *Leading Change* by John Kotter,[31] presents a methodical, somewhat academic, step-by-step approach to the subject. Just follow the steps, and the likelihood of success is enhanced.

The second is much more simplistic, maybe even elementary. The book *Who Moved My Cheese?* by Dr. Spencer Johnson is entertaining and very relatable. It uses the analogy of mice developing a routine

---

31   John Kotter, *Leading Change* (Harvard Business Review Press, 2012).

to get their daily allotment of cheese … until somebody moves the cheese.[32] Like mice, humans can get stuck in ruts and develop comfortable routines … until conditions change.

Navigating through change also emphasizes the CEO's connection with employees. It means that "management by walking around" creates trust among the staff. In the words of one of my colleagues, this may be "*the* most important" task of a CEO, but one of the most difficult to achieve. Other pressing issues and higher priorities often get in the way. There are just so many hours in a day.[33]

PATIENT SAFETY

Herein lies the major difference between healthcare leaders and most business leaders.

We must note that while many industries create highly technical products that demand the highest level of perfection possible, a healthcare executive confronts life-and-death decisions almost daily.

In the early 1980s, I had the opportunity to visit Pennsylvania Hospital, our nation's first hospital, while on a trip to evaluate a medical-records computer system.

During my visit, I took a tour of the original hospital building, which opened in 1751. I recall learning about its rich history and mission of providing quality patient care. That visit to Pennsylvania Hospital left an impression on me, almost as if I were walking on

---

32   Spencer Johnson, *Who Moved My Cheese?* (G. P. Putnam's Sons, 1999).

33   Carl Lindberg, "Management by Walking Around Explained by a CEO," Leadershipahoy, accessed October 23, 2024, https://www.leadershipahoy.com/management-by-walking-around-explained-by-a-ceo/.

hallowed ground. More importantly, its mission of providing quality care was etched into my mind and made me proud to work in an endeavor founded on that core principle.

Over the years, however, the US healthcare system has been repeatedly criticized for its lack of focus on quality. According to some, the entire healthcare system has become complacent and needs a wake-up call related to patient safety.

By the end of the 1990s, higher expectations were placed on hospitals to ensure that patients received the level of care they deserved. There was a heightened emphasis on patient safety. Almost simultaneously, but not necessarily coordinated, two major developments served to address these concerns.

CRUCIBLE #6A:
THE LEAPFROG GROUP

The Leapfrog Group was formed in 2000 as a nonprofit watchdog organization supported by large companies increasingly concerned about the quality of care provided in US hospitals. Fueling these concerns was a study released in 1999 by the Institute of Medicine (known today as the National Academy of Medicine), which estimated that approximately 98,000 people died each year from medical errors occurring in hospitals. Through the efforts of the Leapfrog Group, corporate America was essentially saying that "enough is enough."[34]

---

34 Leapfrog Group, accessed July 29, 2024, https://www.leapfroggroup.org.

CRUCIBLE #6B:

JCAHO NATIONAL PATIENT
SAFETY GOALS PROGRAM

A newly revised set of patient safety standards was adopted in 2002 by the Joint Commission on Accreditation of Healthcare Organizations (JCAHO, known today as the Joint Commission). This new set of standards was established to address patient safety issues and assist healthcare organizations in establishing a framework for improving patient care.[35]

Hospitals became highly prioritized when allocating the resources necessary to ensure compliance with Joint Commission and Leapfrog Group standards. Most already had a department of dedicated staff whose primary responsibility was to implement and monitor ongoing process improvement and organizational effectiveness initiatives. In many cases, the new expectations and heightened awareness related to patient safety meant that even more resources (staff, computer technology, outside consulting services, etc.) might be warranted.

The financial pressures placed on hospitals to make such investments grew even more. Yet the importance of such initiatives was imperative. Just like in the early days at Pennsylvania Hospital, the focus on providing quality patient care should be fundamental to the purpose of all healthcare.

For some hospitals, this required a paradigm shift. Through no fault of those in hospital leadership positions, much of their attention had been directed toward dealing with reimbursement challenges,

---

35   The Joint Commission, "National Patient Safety Goals," accessed July 29, 2024, https://www.jointcommission.org/standards/national-patient-safety-goals/.

keeping up with new technology, workforce issues, and expanding services. It was almost as if the quality of care was assumed.

Yet, in many cases, the oversight and monitoring of measurable patient-care metrics weren't well developed. Improving patient care and addressing patient safety had to be intentional and made a priority of every hospital across America. If the Ford Motor Company could boast that "Quality Is Job One," the same should be true for hospitals.

The evolution of quality initiatives took on an even greater level of importance when CMS announced that quality-performance metrics would be publicly available information. In the blink of an eye, the public could access hospital performance indicators online. Everything from surgical outcomes and hospital-acquired infections to readmission and death rates could be accessed with the click of a mouse.

The stakes of the game rose exponentially. Not only was Big Brother watching, but so was everyone else in the family. The oversight of hospital performance was no longer restricted to medical staff committees and boards of directors. Anyone with the propensity to do so could access hospital-specific information.

Lists of the "Top 100 Best Hospitals" and the "Top 100 Worst Hospitals" began to be published. Hospitals were now operating in a fishbowl, and the public had a front-row seat.

So, the US movement of healthcare quality is multifaceted. Depending on who is asked, publicly available information could be a good thing or a bad thing. That topic can be debated from various points of view, and opinions vary depending on which side of the table one is sitting on. Irrespective of who is right or who is wrong, the horse is already out of the barn. Technology and elevated public interest have brought hospital performance information to the forefront.

Other business sectors have experienced similar oversight. For healthcare leaders, it is another development that requires attention and focus. The quality of care provided at individual institutions can no longer be assumed. It must be monitored, tracked, and documented on an ongoing basis. Gone are the days of doing retrospective studies and gathering outdated information. It is a new day in terms of standard operating procedures.

Doctors passionately trying to solve the complex problems in healthcare rallied. Perhaps one of the most compelling books was the breakthrough *ProvenCare: How to Deliver Value-Based Healthcare the Geisinger Way*, released in 2018 by Glenn D. Steele, MD, and David T. Feinberg, MD. When it comes to providing high-quality care in the most efficient, cost-effective way possible, *ProvenCare* has proven to be the gold standard in the hospital field.

"Developed at Geisinger Health System and praised by healthcare leaders worldwide, this pioneering approach provides an essential blueprint for healthcare executives who want to provide higher levels of care for their patients, greater incentives for practitioners, and smarter solutions at lower costs."[36]

For me, this book shed new light on the importance of delivering cost-efficient care without compromising on quality. Sometimes the most obvious is right before our eyes. Throughout my career, I struggled with the notion of balancing cost and quality. My narrow perspective assumed that quality would inherently suffer when costs were cut. After reading *ProvenCare,* I now have a more enlightened perspective.

Just as leaders in business and industry have embraced quality, healthcare has done so with fervor, knowing full well that this is an indisputable mandate.

---

36   Glenn D. Steele and David T. Feinberg, *ProvenCare: How to Deliver Value-Based Healthcare the Geisinger Way* (McGraw Hill, 2017).

COMPASSIONATE LEADERSHIP

The news I shared about the power of the Leapfrog Group and the Joint Commission patient safety actions may not have registered as a tidal change in folks' minds. But it was. Here were two of the most powerful groups in the country screaming at hospitals to get it right. There are now digital tools to prevent medication errors. There are processes to prevent medical mistakes.

We are no longer accepting excuses. And yes, a lot of hospitals have a lot of catching up to do. And most certainly, this should be done with great joy because lives will be saved in every hospital in the nation.

I believe this was the beginning of compassionate leadership in this country, the moment the mission to *improve health and save lives* overcame finance and complacency, and many of my colleagues would agree.

PART THREE

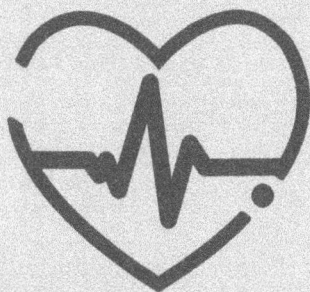

CHAPTER 10

A DIFFERENT STYLE OF LEADERSHIP

> *"Culture" is often used to describe an organization's personality. Like humans, every organization has unique characteristics, and the Baptist Health System was no different.*

M y move back to Knoxville had to be staged. I was to start my new job with the Baptist Health System in early March 2001. But having been away from Knoxville for seventeen and a half years meant that my wife and I had acquired more personal belongings and the usual stuff that families accumulate over time. We also had a house to sell and needed to find a new one.

The biggest challenge, however, centered around our children. While in Middle Tennessee, we added three new little ones to our family. Because of their age differences, our children were in three different levels of school: elementary, middle, and high school. This meant that the area where we chose to live was somewhat driven by school districts and the school's proximity to our neighborhood preferences.

We were also sensitive to the timing of the move. With less than three months remaining in the school year, we decided to wait until school was out to move the family. Since I needed to start my new job earlier, I needed to find temporary housing until the big move could be scheduled.

Everything seemed to go as planned; I moved into an apartment under a four-month lease, hoping that a more permanent option could be found within that time. We put our home in Clarksville on the market, hoping its sale timing would work in our favor. For the next few months, I alternated going to Clarksville every other weekend while my wife and children came to Knoxville on alternate weekends.

Just as I felt good about the job opportunity, things on the family front seemed to fall into place. We found a new home under construction and made an offer. Within a few weeks, we also received an offer on our house in Clarksville. We were able to close on both the sale and purchase and scheduled the big move for mid-July.

As can be expected, we were facing some other huge adjustments. Although we were fortunate to find a home in our preferred school district, we were still faced with helping our children adjust. All three of them, with different degrees of emotion, left friends behind in Clarksville. It was probably most challenging for our oldest, entering the tenth grade. He had to say goodbye to friends he had known since kindergarten. Our middle daughter was entering eighth grade and had to deal with similar separation anxieties, although to a lesser degree. Our youngest was going into the fourth grade. Life was mostly fun and games for her, so the transition wasn't nearly as traumatic.

The bigger challenge came with the new school year in August. All three kids went to new schools where they essentially knew no one. It was a bit frightening at first, but all three grew more comfortable with each passing day.

ADJUSTMENT TO A NEW COMMUNITY

I had similar adjustments to make. Like our children, I had to develop new professional relationships and adjust to a new organizational culture, and it wasn't always easy for me either. Baptist Hospital opened its doors in Knoxville in 1948 and enjoyed a rich heritage and history. The hospital was a fixture of the Knoxville community, located on the south side of the Tennessee River just across from downtown Knoxville.

Its campus had become a landmark, and everyone knew where Baptist Hospital was because of its prominence along that South Knoxville waterfront. To some, it was seen as South Knoxville's preferred hospital because of its location. For many people living south of the river, the mere thought of driving across the bridge to downtown was a mental block.

Like many hospitals, Baptist Hospital's campus had expanded several times over the years with new office buildings and patient wings. The main 1948 building had been refurbished but was still a somewhat dated structure. Other additions also showed wear and tear and needed to be renovated. But, in comparison to other hospitals built during that era, the overall campus was in pretty good shape. Still, the need for ongoing improvements was always at the top of the capital budget wish list.

When I arrived in 2001, the Knoxville healthcare market was in transition. Because the demographics of the greater metropolitan area were shifting, and more people were beginning to move to outlying areas, the need for healthcare services concentrated in the downtown area was slowly declining. Downtown Knoxville had historically been the centerpiece of healthcare services.

Four major downtown hospitals were located within a few miles of each other, along with a stand-alone children's hospital. All four major hospitals had developed their respective regional hospital networks. Competition among the "big four" was intense and getting more so by the day. Each health system was jockeying for position and working hard to grow its market share.

There was a prevailing feeling within the healthcare community that Knoxville was overbedded. The four major hospitals were all licensed for around five hundred beds and were built when inpatient services were the rule rather than the exception. As the community's demographics shifted and the delivery of healthcare services transitioned toward outpatient care, there were more beds in the community than needed. As a result, all four hospital systems were operating fewer beds than their licensed capacity.

To address this issue, Baptist and the other competing health systems looked for opportunities to expand into other areas of the region. Just before I arrived in Knoxville, Baptist had obtained a certificate of need to build a new hospital in West Knoxville. Then, following a series of new filings and public hearings, Baptist was granted final approval to build a new hospital campus that would operate under two separate licenses: ninety beds dedicated to general acute care and sixteen beds dedicated solely to women's services.

As part of this expansion, an equivalent number of beds would be delicensed from the downtown campus and reallocated to the new campus. The new hospital would give the Baptist Health System a new, state-of-the-art facility, and the system would establish a presence in a rapidly growing area of town. It would also reduce the number of licensed beds in the overcrowded downtown market.

The approval process for the new hospital had been challenging and anything but routine. A competing health system already had a significant presence in that part of the community and had added a growing number of new programs and services. There were questions about whether another hospital was needed in that location. Depending on who was asked, it was a brilliant strategic move by Baptist or a poorly conceived idea.

And like many such decisions, for every action, there was an equal and opposite reaction. Thus, as an expected consequence, the approval given to Baptist added yet another log to the already blazing fire of intense competition.

In the early 2000s, the Baptist Health System of East Tennessee consisted of the main Baptist Hospital in downtown Knoxville and three outlying rural hospitals. The new hospital would make it a five-hospital system. While I participated in planning meetings related to the new hospital, my job responsibilities were primarily focused on the central facility downtown.

Like in every other job, I spent the first few months meeting people and learning about the organization, and I enjoyed the same honeymoon period I had experienced at other hospitals. Everyone was very welcoming and gracious. Baptist Hospital had been recognized nationally as a "Top 100 Hospital," and there was optimism about the future. The excitement of building a new hospital further accentuated that optimistic feeling.

HARSH REALITIES

But some harsh realities were lingering in the shadows. A long list of facility concerns at the downtown campus had to be addressed. The fifty-three-year-old core structure had ongoing issues, some requiring immediate attention. There were additional concerns about the more recent additions to the campus. Then, there was the usual and ever-growing list of clinical technology requests that were expected (sometimes demanded) by the medical staff. I can vividly recall my first budget session and the sticker shock of capital improvements that had been identified.

While the new hospital project generated excitement, it also posed a dilemma in terms of resource allocation. How much should the system continue to invest in the downtown facility? Should the new hospital project be given a higher priority and be the preferred strategy to upgrade facilities, equipment, and services?

In some respects, the downtown facility started being looked upon as the proverbial redheaded stepchild. I found myself having to go to bat for improvements downtown that were not only desirable but imperative.

Within a few short months, my plate was full, and time management became a challenge. I found myself balancing normal day-to-day operations with employee and medical staff meetings, while at the same time keeping a watchful eye on the ever-changing local healthcare landscape. Along with other strategic initiatives, the new hospital project demanded some of my time.

Then, to top it off, I needed to devote sufficient time to my family's needs, adjusting to a new home, and building important community relationships. Every waking hour was filled with juggling critical issues.

Another interesting development emerged that had operational and competitive implications. As described in the previous chapter, there were growing concerns about the quality of patient care in hospitals across the US. Patients, patients' families, insurers, and major corporations united to voice these concerns. There was a prevailing perception that the general population was receiving substandard care compared to the price they paid for those services.

The Leapfrog Group, which by now had gained significant national credibility, insisted that hospitals make significant improvements in quality. Every hospital across the US was put on notice. Then, in 2002, the Joint Commission published a new set of quality standards as part of its National Patient Safety Goals program.

Baptist Hospital had a well-developed and well-functioning quality-improvement program. We had a core group of very competent staff and didn't necessarily see the list of Leapfrog expectations and Joint Commission standards to be insurmountable. However, accomplishing them would require a significant investment of resources, not the least of which would be major upgrades in information technology. The price tag and hours necessary to make this happen would be extensive.

Nevertheless, our team knew it was the right thing to do, so a plan was drafted, and efforts to comply were initiated. We also recognized that all other hospitals in our area would implement similar initiatives. Thus, from a competitive standpoint, the pressure to keep up with the competition was also a consideration.

CULTURAL ADJUSTMENTS

The term "culture" is often used to describe an organization's personality. Like humans, every organization has unique characteristics, and the Baptist Health System was no different.

More than any other hospital where I had worked, Baptist was like one big family, and I mean that as a compliment.

A culture of caring was evident everywhere you turned. I had never experienced the degree to which everyone supported everyone. To be fair, I do not wish to disparage the culture of other hospitals where I have worked. Each one of them had a similar family feeling. However, the culture of the Baptist Health System was unique.

I sincerely believe that its faith-based mission and core principles contributed to these differences. Compassion for others was evident everywhere you turned. The organization's mission was based on Christian beliefs and principles, and it showed. It didn't take long to realize that I was fortunate to work alongside many dedicated staff. In many respects, their calling of service superseded everything else. They truly cared for the whole person.

Each patient's emotional and spiritual well-being was equally as important as their physical well-being. That caring spirit was on display every day, whether attending to the needs of patients or each other. All meetings began with prayer, and individual prayer requests were shared publicly. It was not uncommon to see chaplains, physicians, and other staff members praying with patients and families during especially stressful times.

I felt very comfortable with Baptist's caring culture. Conversely, however, that culture was a bit intimidating. For newcomers like me, it took a while to understand the nuances of such a deep-seated "big family" culture and to figure out how to fit in. I was confident that my values aligned with those of the organization, but I was uncertain of how others perceived me. I hoped that I could live up to their expectations. Among the growing issues already on my plate, adjusting to the culture probably posed one of my most significant challenges. And I may have underestimated how challenging it would be.

I have followed several long-tenured leaders in my career. In each case, it took time to establish my style and gain the organization's trust (i.e., the *25-50-25* rule). When I joined Baptist, I followed a very seasoned and respected leader, but the situation differed from all the others. My predecessor at Baptist didn't have a quarter-century tenure, as was the case at the other hospitals.

However, he was extremely bright, competent, and successful. He had received numerous awards, including a national honor as ACHE Young Healthcare Executive of the Year. He had earned high respect from his peers throughout the state and the nation. The Top 100 Hospital recognition that Baptist had received was primarily attributed to his leadership. Some referred to him as a rock star, and one person described him as "one of the smartest people I have ever known."

My leadership style, personality, and demeanor vastly differed from his. I was more people oriented, and he was more results oriented. I had my strengths, but I found it very challenging to live up to the standards that he had set. He had established an impressive track record of success, and it was a hard act to follow. The 25 percent who welcomed change supported me and did everything they could to make my transition easy. At the opposite end of the spectrum, however, was the 25 percent who wanted me to be a clone of my predecessor. They respected his leadership style and expected me to be like him. This included employees, managers, physicians, and board members.

When I first started in my new position, I solicited input from all perspectives, but I didn't feel the immediate need to change my style or approach. My leadership style had already been established, and at that stage in my career, I'm not sure if I could have changed my style even if I had wanted to.

Some failed to recognize that the healthcare landscape was also very different and changing daily. The Knoxville healthcare community was transitioning, and competition among hospital systems was intensifying. Every hospital system was looking to expand, including investment in new facilities and equipment, aggressive physician recruitment, and access to insurance networks. But the overall pie was shrinking, and it was evident that there may not be room for everyone.

The new hospital project had added another element of complexity to an already complex environment, and financial pressures mounted. Baptist was challenged with maintaining operations at the downtown campus, making the necessary investments in infrastructure and equipment while allocating sufficient manpower and resources to the new hospital.

Physicians were growing anxious, wondering how the changing environment would affect their practices. Some questioned when or if they may need to relocate their offices. As would be expected, physicians wanted to be assured that they were hitching their wagon to a successful partner.

As a result, the first eighteen months in my job were anything but routine. The term "perfect storm" may be overdramatic, but it seems fitting. I found myself juggling multiple variables, and I had little control over many of them. However, I can summarize the key issues into three main categories.

1. **Increased Competition**

   Increased competition among hospitals and changes within the local healthcare landscape added to the pressures. The shift toward outpatient services, a declining need for hospital beds in the downtown area, population migration to the outlying areas, and evolving insurance networks.

2. **Market Position**

   Baptist's overall market position and the challenges the new hospital project brought. Among Knoxville's four major health systems, Baptist was fourth in size and market share. The new hospital was a strategic decision to move into a new area and grow market share. It made strategic sense; however, the timing of the new hospital and the other changes in the local healthcare community put significant financial strain on the system.

3. **Cultural Adjustments**

The cultural adjustments of joining a new organization and the challenges of following a strong, well-respected, and successful leader. As I reflect on those first eighteen months at Baptist, this is the area where I would second-guess myself the most. I have confidence in my knowledge and expertise, but I am not sure my leadership style was the right fit. I never did win over the 25 percent who preferred my predecessor's leadership style. Then again, given the rapidly changing healthcare environment, perhaps my timing was also bad.

REASSIGNMENT OF DUTIES

As the financial pressures continued to mount, leadership changes were made within the Baptist System. The duties and responsibilities of several executives changed, and some were reassigned to new positions. That included me. I moved into the corporate office and took on a new role, which included responsibility for several system-wide departments and administrative liaison with the three outlying hospitals. A mandatory senior management team-building initiative followed.

Under the guidance of a professional facilitator, we began scheduling monthly meetings to improve overall team performance. The book *Good to Great* by Jim Collins[37] was required reading for this

---

37   Jim Collins, *Good to Great* (Harper Business, 2001).

initiative. It served as an outline for discussion topics and provided insight from other successful companies. Interestingly, Jim Collins had coauthored *Built to Last*, the book I had read years before as part of the planning process in Clarksville.

Initially, I felt out of place in my new role, but I grew more comfortable as I developed new relationships. The most fulfilling aspect of my new responsibilities was the opportunity to work with the community hospitals. It took me back to my days in Gallatin and Clarksville. The phrase "neighbors caring for neighbors" characterized the culture of those hospitals. It was a much different environment from the highly competitive environment of the big city.

I divided my time between the corporate office and visits to each hospital. Those visits included monthly medical staff and board meetings at all three facilities. As a result, I spent significant time in my car with lots of time to think. With each passing day, there was a growing sense of uncertainty, and I wasn't sure what the future would hold.

In some ways, I was waiting for the next shoe to fall. Then it happened, and it happened under a most surreal set of circumstances.

COMPASSIONATE LEADERSHIP

I would have bet money that the culture of the Baptist Health System would win the day. A family atmosphere, a spiritual calling, a great community. But you could read the tea leaves. Once a community fears losing a hospital, once the leadership becomes concerned about the future, the cloud of uncertainty prevails. No management style can overcome the forces at play. Boards are made up of business leaders who do not ever want to see anything but dramatic success on the balance sheet. When a community has too many beds and too many hospitals, one or more will disappear. Competition. It sounds very American, but in practical observation, competition is a double-edged sword. This happened in markets across America. And it's still happening.

CHAPTER 11

MY DAY OF INFAMY

I didn't recognize the number, so I ignored the call, allowing it to go to voicemail. Once the meeting concluded, I called my voicemail and listened to a concise but alarming message.

"Mr. Decker, this is an emergency. Please call me back at your earliest opportunity."

Prepared for the worst, I hung up and immediately redialed the number showing on my phone. At that moment, an already eventful day just got worse.

When my responsibilities within the Baptist Health System changed, I assumed administrative oversight of the three outlying community hospitals, including the Baptist Hospital of Cocke County in Newport, Tennessee. The drive from my home in Knoxville to Newport took about one hour, mostly via Interstate 40. There is one stretch of highway where the interstate veers slightly east and crosses Douglas Lake, one of several lakes within the Tennessee Valley Authority waterway system.

The scenery is breathtaking as you cross the bridge and head toward North Carolina, especially during certain seasons. The lake has a natural beauty, and the Smoky Mountains can be seen on the horizon as you drive eastward. If you time it right, you can witness a magnificent early-morning sunrise. Quite frankly, I enjoyed that morning drive and took advantage of the hour of solitude to take in the scenery along the way.

Newport is very similar to other cities of its size in the southern Appalachian region. Nestled against the backdrop of the Great Smoky Mountains, it is the county seat of Cocke County and is considered one of the state's most beautiful regions. With a population of around seven thousand, it has a typical small-town charm, brimming with tradition and notoriety. Depending on who is asked, its citizens are either warm and friendly, or downright mean.

During my brief tenure there, I encountered some of both. Cocke County has stable businesses, strong churches, committed leaders, and tremendous community pride. It also has a history of cockfighting, gambling, and illegal moonshining, which sometimes tarnishes its reputation.

The hospital also has a fascinating history. Although hard to believe, there were once two hospitals in this small community. One was a private hospital founded by local physicians. It had been very successful over the years and enjoyed tremendous community support, attributed to the community's respect for those physicians. The second hospital was county owned and, over time, was viewed as the indigent hospital for the region.

In 1983, the Baptist Health System assumed management of the county hospital. After conducting its due diligence, Baptist purchased the hospital from the county and facilitated a merger with the private hospital to avoid duplication of services and create economies of scale. A deal was consummated through negotiations involving various public and private entities, leading to the consolidation of services on one campus. The resulting Cocke County Baptist Hospital (later renamed Baptist Hospital of Cocke County, or simply BHCC) began operating under one consolidated license.

Because my position within the Baptist Health System included a variety of system-wide duties and responsibilities, my primary office remained in the corporate office suite at the main campus in Knoxville. I would schedule my visits to Newport and the other two hospitals in advance, depending on the priorities of each facility. This meant I would generally drive to Newport once or twice a month. I would attend monthly management meetings, board meetings, and medical staff meetings.

I can't honestly attest to how I was perceived by the people there, but I suspect that some saw me as a helpful liaison between the system and the local hospital. Others, however, most likely saw me as an outsider from the big city. They weren't sure if I was there to help or to hinder. I found myself, once again, having to build trust.

I would characterize my relationships with the CEOs at all three hospitals as positive. They welcomed my input on complex issues and respected my advice. They also knew I would advocate for them at the system level regarding budget requests and resource allocation. I worked hard to earn their trust. Their needs differed from those of the larger hospitals within the system, but that didn't mean they were any less important. I was committed to preserving that balanced perspective.

Two key developments emerged as I got comfortable with my new responsibilities and balanced my time between Knoxville and the outlying hospitals. Somewhat unanticipatedly, the CEO at BHCC resigned abruptly. He had been in that position for over twenty years and was a popular and respected community leader. He initiated several new programs and services and spearheaded building expansion projects.

His resignation surprised the hospital staff and the community. Almost overnight, I had to deal with a prevailing sense of anxiety and uncertainty. Consequently, my schedule had to be adjusted, and I spent more time than usual in Cocke County.

I was appointed BHCC's interim CEO a few days after the previous CEO's resignation. Initially, my primary focus was to stabilize and support. With the growing uncertainty of the Baptist Health System's future and the sudden departure of a long-tenured CEO, the staff and physicians at Cocke County were understandably concerned.

Rumors began to circulate about what would or wouldn't happen. Employees feared losing their jobs, and the community feared losing its hospital. I took on the role of a caretaker and calming presence in a raging storm.

Truth be known, I was as concerned about the future as everyone else. My stomach was in knots, and I wasn't sure how things would turn out. Outwardly, however, I tried hard to convey a spirit of optimism. The often-used phrase "Never let them see you sweat" certainly rang true.

While the challenge seemed daunting, I embraced the moment and went to work. I held weekly meetings with department heads to keep them informed. I held employee meetings on all three shifts and spent additional time making rounds throughout the hospital. Very little of my time was spent in my office at my desk. I wanted to get to know the employees, and I wanted them to see me as approachable.

The most important thing was to show them that I cared. I prioritized empathizing with what they had been through and demonstrating a willingness to walk alongside them. Interestingly, I sensed they were hungry for compassion, and it didn't take long to figure that out. I began each day by greeting, welcoming, and encouraging the staff. They needed to know that they were valued and appreciated.

Throughout my education, training, and experience, the importance of open communication had been reinforced repeatedly. Now was the time to put it to the test. As time progressed, I started to build trust among the staff, and I sensed that we were beginning to develop a bond. I was viewed as an outsider since I didn't live in the community, but people eventually warmed up to me. I felt appreciated.

The medical staff was a bit more challenging. Much like my experiences at other hospitals, the *25-50-25* rule came into play. The former CEO had garnered a great deal of support among many of the long-term physicians. That was understandable, given the twenty years they had worked together. Conversely, a significant number of physicians were encouraged by the change in leadership. They felt that a fresh set of eyes and ears could be healthy for the organization.

I made a special effort to spend time with all physicians, regardless of their preconceived mindsets. Most physician offices were either on the hospital campus or within walking distance, making it very convenient for me. I scheduled face-to-face meetings with each physician to assure them that I was there to work in everyone's best interests. Some believed me; others were more skeptical. All expressed appreciation for the personal visit.

As in my meetings with employees, I sensed that the physicians also needed some TLC. To a degree, they had felt neglected and perceived that their concerns had been ignored. I made it a priority to show them that I cared. I was amazed at how a genuine dose of compassion can go a long way in building relationships. It took time, but I eventually earned their trust.

Since the Baptist Health System owned BHCC, it did not have a separate board with governance authority. However, it did have an advisory board composed of community leaders and governmental officials, some of whom had been on the board of the county hospital.

I found that they were very supportive of the hospital and wanted to do all they could to help. They supported me from day one and never questioned that I wasn't a resident of Cocke County. Granted, they all had opinions of the hospital and what needed to be done, but they all pledged their support. Within a very short period, I had developed a new circle of friends and professional contacts.

Earlier, I described the Baptist Health System as one big family. As an extension of that theme, BHCC could be described as a "clan" within the larger family. While most employees, physicians, and board members appreciated being part of the Baptist family, they sometimes felt underappreciated. Very simply, one size doesn't always fit all. Rural hospitals' issues and challenges differ from those at metropolitan medical centers. My job was to bridge the gap.

In addition to my interim duties in Cocke County, I continued to allocate time for other responsibilities. I still made trips to the two other outlying hospitals, but less frequently. I also continued with other system-level departmental oversight. Balancing those responsibilities was challenging, but somehow, I managed. I developed a routine that seemed to work well and devoted sufficient time to all assigned duties.

SUMMONED TO THE CORNER OFFICE

That routine changed abruptly one morning when I was summoned to a meeting with the CEO of the Baptist Health System. At that meeting, I was informed that an outside consulting firm had been retained to help address the system's declining financial performance. With this consulting engagement, several executives would be reassigned to different areas, and a team of consultants would be deployed to focus on specific issues.

This meant that my responsibilities would also be changing. Because it was important to maintain continuity of leadership in Cocke County, I was assigned to BHCC full time. The "interim" title was removed, and I became CEO. My other duties and responsibilities were reassigned to other senior management team members.

Those one-hour morning commutes to Cocke County became my daily routine. Depending on my schedule for the day, I would leave home early enough to allow for the long drive to Newport. Frequently, I was expected to be at the hospital for 7:00 a.m. medical staff meetings, so I would need to be on the road by 6:00 a.m. It was not uncommon for there to be two or three such meetings each week.

At the end of the day, my goal was to leave my office around 6:00 p.m., allowing for late-afternoon meetings or necessary office work. Once at home, usually at 7:00 p.m. or later, I would do my best to decompress, eat dinner, enjoy some family time, and reflect on the day's activities. Then, the next day, I would do it all over again.

As is true in any rural community, the hospital CEO is a very visible figure. Within a few short weeks, I was invited to speak to civic clubs, community gatherings, and Chamber of Commerce meetings. Everyone in the community was interested in what was going on at the hospital. I welcomed those opportunities and used them to provide credible information and cultivate meaningful relationships.

After about six months, I was appointed to the board of directors of the Newport Chamber of Commerce and the board of the Boys and Girls Club, and I was selected to participate in the Leadership Cocke County program. Even though I still resided in Knoxville, I felt welcomed as an honorary citizen of Cocke County.

Not only did my involvement in these organizations help to build community support for the hospital, but it also gave me a much better understanding of community needs. I developed a much deeper appreciation for the people of the area, especially those dealing with challenging circumstances. I used this as an opportunity to build relationships and friendships that continue to this day. More importantly, I used the opportunity to reevaluate my priorities and unleash a leadership style that emphasizes care and compassion.

But those community activities added even more pressure to my daily routine. Most meetings and events were after business hours, lengthening my day further. Those routine twelve-plus-hour days quickly ballooned to fourteen-plus-hour days, putting more stress on my car and my physical stamina. To borrow a commonly used phrase, I was "burning the candle at both ends."

I knew the pace was unsustainable, so I got creative with time management. One of the community leaders I had met was the owner/operator of the local Holiday Inn motel. After attending a community event, she expressed concern that I was spending so much time on the road, driving back and forth between Knoxville and Newport.

She proposed an arrangement whereby I could stay overnight at the Holiday Inn at a discounted rate on the days of those late-night/early-morning turnarounds. A master account was developed, and a monthly bill was sent to the hospital for the nights I stayed at the motel. It was a great arrangement and alleviated the wear and tear on my body. It is incredible what a good night's sleep can do for one's mental alertness.

A PROJECT TO KEEP ME FOCUSED

One of the more challenging projects I tackled at BHCC involved a building expansion to enlarge the emergency department. This project was already in the planning stages before my arrival. The existing emergency department was too small to adequately handle a growing volume of patients, resulting in inefficient patient flow. Funding for the project had supposedly been included in the capital budget.

The original plans called for a two-story addition, with the basement level devoted to expanded space for classrooms and storage space. The main level was designed to add more emergency-treatment cubicles and ancillary support. The hospital staff, physicians, and a team of architects had worked for months to arrive at a final set of drawings. The assumption would be that the project would proceed as envisioned.

With the planning process essentially complete, I was faced with shepherding the project through the approval process in Knoxville. However, it soon became apparent that a project of this scale and magnitude had little chance of being approved. With the system's other financial challenges, such a financial commitment wasn't looked upon favorably.

In one meeting, when I first presented the project background, rationale, and concept, I was told to scrap the project. It simply wasn't going to fly.

Suddenly, I was reminded of a saying that a professional colleague first introduced to me during my administrative residency years before. He told me that sometimes things don't always go as expected, and you will feel "rammed by the rigid rod of reality." With my tail between my legs, I returned to the drawing board.

I was the one to break the bad news to the staff and physicians at BHCC. They had been led to believe that the project would proceed as planned. Their disappointment was expected and, quite frankly, understandable. Suddenly, the Baptist Health System became the villain, and I was the easiest target.

I had to deal with the backlash, and verbal criticism of what they felt was a broken promise. This further reinforced their perception that BHCC always drew the short end of the stick. Emotions were boiling, and spirits were demoralized. I had a mess on my hands.

Once the waters calmed and emotions cooled, I scheduled a meeting with the hospital's management team and key physicians. I knew I had to be the voice of reason and maintain a sense of balanced perspectives. The reality was the project could not proceed as planned. However, I felt strongly that the project's primary goal to expand the emergency department still had merit. The increasing volume of emergency patients could not be ignored.

That argument was easily documented by analyzing emergency-visit trends over the past several years and projected population growth. I was convinced that the hospital's reputation and service to the community would be jeopardized if something wasn't done to alleviate the overcrowding in the emergency department. I was also optimistic (with my fingers crossed behind my back) that I could sell this at the system level, but the project's scope would need to change.

After a lengthy and somewhat heated discussion, we agreed to proceed with a modified, scaled-down version of the project. We eliminated the entire basement level from the plans and focused on the improvements needed in the emergency department. We established a new project timeline, allowing sufficient time to meet with the architects and interested parties. The project, at least for now, was back on track.

Within a few short weeks, we had a revised plan with revised cost estimates. By being more personally invested in the project through the revision process, I felt even more convinced that the project was needed. We had done our homework, had realistic expectations, and had a solid, defensible plan to present for consideration. A meeting in Knoxville was scheduled, and I was prepared for virtually any question that could come my way.

I saw this as my project, and the outcome rested on my shoulders. I was convinced that it was needed for the community and, just as important, to demonstrate support for the staff and physicians. Our efforts and hard work were appreciated and applauded. The project was approved with few questions or concerns, and we were given the green light to proceed. It was one of those moments to celebrate, which we did as only Cocke County can do.

I viewed this as a huge win for the hospital and an even bigger win for the community. On a personal level, it was a massive win for me as well. Almost every day for the next several months during the site preparation and construction process, employees, physicians, and community citizens would seek me out to voice their excitement over the new emergency department. It had been several years since the hospital had untaken an expansion project of this size, and it was the buzz of the town. The excitement was palpable. It also served to calm some of the fears and concerns about the hospital's future.

Meanwhile, the consultants were working hard behind the scenes. They identified a few areas that needed attention, and we developed a plan to implement their recommendations. For the most part, BHCC was performing well. Some low-hanging fruit was eliminated, and a few other difficult cost reductions were made, but nothing that caused much of an uproar. I felt proud of how our staff responded, especially our management team. There was a spirit of teamwork that seemed to rise to the occasion.

However, the system-wide picture was not nearly as rosy. There continued to be serious concerns about where the Baptist Health System was headed. Expense reductions had been implemented in almost every area of operations, and uncertainty continued to swell. It all came to a head on the gloomy morning of December 8, 2005, the day of the quarterly Baptist Health System board meeting.

As a senior management team member, I was in attendance as usual. The agenda seemed routine enough, with various reports and updates. Then, the board chair asked to go into an executive session and excused all management members except for the system's CEO. We quietly went to the corridor outside the meeting room while the board deliberated privately. I lost track of time, but it seemed like we were in that hallway for an eternity.

We were then called back into the room and informed that the CEO had resigned, and a long-tenured board member was appointed interim CEO. While the news was not necessarily surprising, it still stung.

There were myriad thoughts going through my head. Would I still have a job? Should I start looking for another job? Where do we go from here? What about my family? I was confused and worried.

EVENTFUL DAY JUST GOT WORSE

CRUCIBLE #7:
HEAD-ON COLLISION

December 8, 2005, is a day I will never forget. My wife was involved in a head-on collision, leaving her with multiple fractures and injuries. Understandably, this was a crucible of great significance and easily fits into the category of "Life happens." To say it was life-changing would be an understatement.

Amid the discussion that ensued and my unfocused attempts to process the information, my cell phone started vibrating.

I didn't recognize the number, so I ignored the call, allowing it to go to voicemail.

Once the meeting concluded, I called my voicemail and listened to a concise but alarming message: "Mr. Decker, this is an emergency. Please call me back as soon as possible."

Prepared for the worst, I hung up and immediately redialed the number showing on my phone. At that moment, an already eventful day just got worse.

A gentleman answered my call, and I identified myself as receiving his voicemail message. He remained calm, which I appreciated, but informed me that my wife had been involved in a severe head-on collision and was being transported by ambulance to the trauma unit at the University of Tennessee Medical Center (UTMC). Suddenly, any thoughts about my job security or the future of the Baptist Health System were immaterial.

I became 100 percent focused on her condition and the seriousness of her injuries. Within a few minutes, I was in my car, driving as fast as possible. To this day, I remember nothing about that drive or how long it took to get to the hospital.

I walked into the emergency department, identified myself, and was quickly ushered back to one of the treatment cubicles. I found my wife to be conscious but groggy due to a battery of pain medications. I had a brief conversation with the surgeon, who informed me that she had a broken leg (tibia and fibula) and a dislocated ankle on the other leg. Fortunately, there were no other life-threatening injuries.

I held her hand, hugged her neck, kissed her, and reassured her that she was in good hands. A few minutes later, she was wheeled down the hall to surgery.

An entire book could be written about what occurred over the next several hours, but here is the short version. With adrenaline pumping through my veins at a high speed, I collected my thoughts enough to make all the necessary phone calls. I called family, friends, and loved ones. I called my pastor and the Baptist Hospital chaplain.

Then, like a chain reaction, I started getting phone calls as the news circulated. I received comforting calls offering thoughts and prayers. I received offers to help with our children and pets and to make food arrangements. The outpouring of love and concern humbled me.

I also had to return to a work mindset to deal with a few issues at the hospital. Ordinarily, I would have scheduled a meeting with the BHCC management team to update them on the system's change in leadership. As it turned out, I had to delegate that responsibility to another senior executive.

In the preface of this book, I referenced the term "crucible" to describe significant events and experiences that may alter a leader's course of action and the importance of a leader's adaptive capacity to deal with them. Sometimes, a crucible might be a life-altering event in one's personal life. Some people describe this simply as "Life happens."

I can honestly say that the events of December 8, 2005, were life-altering. They changed the way I look at myself and other people. I don't see either in the same light as before. The irony of that day is that it occurred on the sixty-fourth anniversary of President Franklin D. Roosevelt's famous "Day of Infamy" speech.

On December 7, 1941, the Japanese bombed Pearl Harbor and forever altered the course of World War II. As US citizens would never again think of America as isolated and peaceful, my view of my career and myself changed on December 8, 2005. It was my Day of Infamy.

I share the transcript of that historic speech. Reading the Pearl Harbor speech evokes the feelings I had the morning of my wife's accident. Shock. Anger. Fear. Uncertainty. Determination. The ridiculous stress level of my job faded into meaninglessness. I was focused on this moment.

"A DATE WHICH WILL LIVE IN INFAMY"

From the transcript of President Roosevelt's speech, which he delivered in Washington, DC, on December 8, 1941—one day after the assault:

As Commander in Chief of the Army and Navy, I have directed that all measures be taken for our defense. But always will our whole nation remember the character of the onslaught against us.

No matter how long it may take us to overcome this pre-meditated invasion, the American people in their righteous might will win through to absolute victory.

I believe that I interpret the will of the Congress and of the people when I assert that we will not only defend ourselves to the uttermost but will make it very certain that this form of treachery shall never again endanger ...

I ask that the Congress declare that since the unprovoked and dastardly attack by Japan on Sunday, December 7th, 1941, a state of war has existed between the United States and the Japanese empire. [38]

---

38 Melissa Chan, "President Roosevelt's Pearl Harbor Address," *TIME* magazine, December 6, 2018, accessed April 21, 2024, https://time.com/4593483/pearl-harbor-franklin-roosevelt-infamy-speech-attack.

I don't profess to have the wisdom or fortitude that President Roosevelt had, especially during that tense and stressful period of time. I can't begin to relate to what he may have been feeling. But in some ways, I was faced with a similar set of circumstances. Like President Roosevelt, I somehow developed the fortitude and resolve to meet the challenges head-on and was prepared to do so no matter how long it may take.

COMPASSIONATE LEADERSHIP

When I look back at the angels we had on our shoulders through this family crisis, from the initial accident to my wife's recovery, I am so grateful to everyone at Baptist, to the first responders, and to the trauma unit at UTMC. I am grateful for my coworkers who understood that my unsustainable management pace, with the future of my family in the balance, was no longer feasible. Perhaps in retrospect, hospital leaders who demand unsustainable six- and seven-day workweeks from their administrators should rethink that ethic.

CHAPTER 12

A CHANGE IN SCENERY

> *I asked him what he knew about the accident and why he was the one to call me. The story he shared over the next several minutes gave me goose bumps.*

A ny thoughts of getting a good night's sleep vanished as the hours passed on that fateful day. There was an eerie, somewhat surreal feeling from which I couldn't escape. In the back of my mind, I remember thinking that this must be a bad dream and that I would eventually wake up and find everything back to normal.

My physical exhaustion was masked by an unrelenting surge of adrenaline. I could neither sit still nor relax. There was just too much uncertainty to process.

A professional colleague at UTMC arranged for me and my children to use one of their private family waiting rooms. Close friends brought us dinner. I can't overstate how comforting it was to have my children with me and to be reassured that they were safe. We ate quietly, anxiously waiting for news from the surgeon.

As expected, my kids were concerned for their mother and asked me questions about the accident. At that moment, I realized that I didn't know many details. When the gentleman called earlier to tell me about the accident, I cut him off abruptly and didn't even thank him for his call. I didn't even know his name.

I was too focused on getting to the hospital to check on my wife's condition. With a sense of guilt, I knew that I needed to call him again, so I redialed his number.

When he answered, I apologized for cutting him off earlier, which he certainly understood. Then, I made sure to get his name.

> *I asked him what he knew about the accident and why he was the one to call me. The story he shared over the next several minutes gave me goose bumps.*

My wife had been to the grocery store and was driving along a two-lane road close to our home. As noted by eyewitnesses and later confirmed by the police report, a driver had veered over into her lane and hit her head-on. She had no time to react.

The gentleman who called was working at a nearby construction site and heard the crash, then immediately ran to the accident to assist. He saw that my wife was pinned inside her car, unable to get free. He first tried to open the driver's side door, but it was jammed shut, so he tried the passenger side.

He opened the door and found my wife conscious, but noticeably shaken. She was pinned behind the steering wheel, and it was apparent that she did not have use of her legs. The airbags had been deployed, which made communication difficult. He was able to reassure her and unbuckle her safety belt, then lifted her over the middle console (she was driving a large SUV) and removed her from the vehicle.

Unfortunately, that stretch of road had very narrow shoulders, so he had to carry her a short distance before finding a suitable place to lay her down. By the grace of God, she was conscious enough to give him my name and phone number.

If the circumstances weren't horrific enough, within a few minutes after he got her settled on the ground, her car burst into flames. That gentleman will forever be our guardian angel. If he had not been close enough to hear the crash and then willing to help, I cannot imagine how things would have turned out.

The surgeon finally emerged from surgery to give us his report. The good news was that the surgery was successful. He was able to repair the broken bones in her right leg and reattach the torn ligaments and tendons of her left ankle. No other major injuries were noted other than some bruising from the tension of the safety belt.

The bad news was that she would have a long road to recovery ahead. She would be kept in the hospital for two nights to allow the nursing staff to monitor her post-op progress, then discharged home in a wheelchair. There would be no weight bearing on either leg for at least three months. She would also leave the hospital with some impressive stitches, staples, and orthopedic hardware.

But she was alive.

I have spent most of my professional career working in hospitals. I know the drill. But other than being with my wife following the birth of our three children, I hadn't spent much time overnight as a hospital visitor. It was foreign to me, and I felt out of place.

I can't remember much about that first night, but I know I didn't get much sleep. It would be easy to blame it on the lumpy lounge chair in my wife's room, but the reality was that I couldn't relax. The events of the day were overwhelming and still swirling in my head.

My wife spent the next three months in a hospital bed in our basement at home. I became her primary caregiver, in addition to scheduled visits by home health nurses and therapists. I arranged my schedule to be at home when the providers came to ensure I was doing everything expected of me.

I was a novice at first, but quickly mastered the necessary duties and tasks. I learned to transfer her from the bed to a wheelchair, and from the wheelchair to our car for follow-up doctor visits. With each passing day, I gained more and more respect for the skill and compassion of healthcare workers.

I also learned to balance my time between my wife's care and my duties at BHCC. That was the hard part. Initially, immediately following the accident, I was able to take a few days off to get her settled at home. I maintained contact with the hospital through phone and email and made myself available if needed.

However, I knew that the change in system leadership would likely create anxiety among hospital employees, so I wanted to be there as soon as possible to provide reassurance. That's when our network of friends and relatives played a vital role. Through their efforts, we assembled a regular rotation of people to come to our home during the daytime hours so I could drive to Newport. It wasn't optimal, but it was the best alternative.

The ensuing three months forced me to adopt a new daily routine and pushed the limits of my comfort zone. In those ninety days, I probably developed more discipline, character, and self-determination than in any other comparable period of my adult life.

My schedule was somewhat rigid, and each minute had to be carefully planned. My two daughters, one in high school and one in middle school, were still living at home, and their assistance in handling household chores was invaluable. We became a well-functioning team as we tended to my wife's needs while juggling school and work priorities.

The uncertainty at work continued to percolate. Soon after the dust settled following the resignation of the system CEO, the board announced that a formal process would be followed to entertain offers from interested parties to purchase the Baptist Health System.

As might be expected, this generated another wave of anxiety among employees and physicians and placed yet another burden on my shoulders. I had to help calm the waters while, at the same time, maintaining daily hospital operations. I had to be laser-focused on the hospital's needs every minute I was on the job.

There was little, if any, time to be concerned about the well-being of my wife. I had to trust that she was being adequately cared for by my network of family, friends, and home health caregivers. By the end of each day, I was physically and emotionally exhausted, and those daily commutes to and from Newport started to wear on me.

TIME FOR A CHANGE

In the early spring of 2006, I knew something had to give. My wife had progressed to the point where she could slowly start managing some weight-bearing activities and begin home health physical therapy. By then, she had also developed a case of cabin fever and was ready for a change in scenery.

I wanted so much to be with her through her rehabilitation journey, but the demands of my job continued to mount. The board had narrowed the list of prospective buyers, and I was expected to assist with site visits and produce the requested information. There were weeks when I couldn't predict what would happen from one day to the next, and there were days when I couldn't predict what would happen from one minute to the next. I felt like I was on a merry-go-round spinning out of control.

As the process progressed, one potential buyer emerged as the lead candidate. The respective parties signed a letter of intent, subject to further due diligence. The intensity of site visits and document production grew even more, and the time required intensified.

Looking back on those days, I want to think that I performed my assigned duties in good faith. As a senior executive, I knew I had a professional and fiduciary responsibility to represent the organization's interests, and I did so to the best of my ability.

In the back of my mind, however, I knew that my job would be in jeopardy if the sale went through. I have been around the block enough times in my career to know that the sale of a hospital or health system often meant a wholesale change in leadership. On top of all the other pressures, the uncertainty of my future started to weigh heavily on my mind.

Then one day, I received an unexpected phone call from an old friend and colleague with whom I had worked years earlier at Fort Sanders. He left Fort Sanders shortly after I did to become CEO of MEDIC Regional Blood Center in Knoxville, but we maintained contact over the years. He had heard the news about my wife's accident through mutual friends and wanted to get an update on the status of her recovery. We also spent a few minutes exchanging pleasantries, reliving old times, and just catching up.

Toward the end of our call, he casually mentioned that he would be retiring as CEO of MEDIC later in the year and was starting to identify potential candidates for his replacement. Ideally, his successor should have at least ten years of experience and a strong leadership background, preferably in a healthcare setting. He asked that if I knew of anyone who might be interested in the job, please pass their names along. The formal search had not yet begun; however, the MEDIC board had asked him to start making a list of names.

I told him I would be happy to help and would let him know if I thought of anyone. I had so many other things on my mind that I didn't give it much thought. Ironically, and although I didn't realize it then, his call planted a seed in my mind that would eventually take me down an entirely new career path.

WHY NOT ME?

Later that evening, after another long and stressful day at work and my one-hour commute home, I had time to reflect on the conversation. It was one of those moments that some people may call "divine intervention."

My wife's recovery was first and foremost in my thoughts, and I felt guilty about not being with her for more than a few hours a day. The stress of my job was increasing, and the daily commutes were taking their toll. The overarching uncertainty of my job and the potential change in ownership of the Baptist Health System was always on my mind.

As I lay in bed that night, staring at the ceiling and trying my best to relax, a small voice kept saying, "Why not me?"

What if I were to apply for the MEDIC job? Is this an opportunity I can't let pass? Strangely, despite being physically and emotionally fatigued, I had a hard time falling asleep. My brain was working overtime, processing the possibilities.

The next morning, as I prepared for another busy day, I briefly talked with my wife about the phone call. I remember telling her I couldn't explain why, but something about the MEDIC opportunity interested me. We didn't have much time to talk, but her initial reaction was supportive. As was true throughout my professional career, she trusted my judgment.

My one-hour commute to Newport that morning seemed to go faster than usual. I used the time to make a mental list of the pros and cons of the MEDIC opportunity. Although I didn't put it in writing, my mental list was something like this:

PROS

- I wouldn't have to move my family. However, I knew that if the Baptist Health System were sold, my job would be in jeopardy. I would then need to seek employment elsewhere, likely in another city. With one child in college, one finishing high school, and one entering high school, I didn't relish the thought.
- I could escape a very precarious situation and exit on my terms. The future of my job and the future of the Baptist Health System were very uncertain. I would welcome going to a more stable organization.
- I would have more time to spend with my wife during her recovery and rehabilitation. I had become somewhat numb to the demands of working in hospitals, and there were no signs of things slowing down. A more predictable work-life balance would be a welcome change.
- MEDIC had a strong and positive reputation in the community. I wouldn't be jumping ship to just any organization. MEDIC was, and still is, a valued community asset.

CONS

- I would be going to a different field. I was confident in my abilities; however, the nuances of the blood industry would require a learning curve.
- My annual salary would likely be less than my current salary. The level of compensation would be different based on the differences between the two organizations.
- I wasn't fully vested in Baptist's retirement plan. Consequently, I would not receive 100 percent of my retirement account balance. This wasn't necessarily a deal breaker, but it was a consideration.
- I didn't want to leave Baptist without a well-defined transition plan. I had too much respect for the organization and too much professional integrity to leave them hanging.

As was my nature, I didn't act too quickly. I needed time to think, have additional conversations with my wife, and fully consider all the implications of making a move. But I also knew that time was ticking. After a few days of thought, soul-searching, and prayer (lots of prayer), I decided to go for it. I called my friend back and told him that I had someone I'd like to recommend. I told him I wanted to throw my hat into the ring.

By midsummer, the MEDIC board began the formal process of interviewing candidates, and I was scheduled to interview with the board chairman and several board members. It must have gone well because I was then scheduled for a follow-up meeting with more board members, including the physician whose vision led to the founding of MEDIC.

A few weeks later, I was offered the position, so I resigned from Baptist, giving them two months' notice. It was important to me to provide such notice because of all the uncertainty within Baptist at that time. As it turned out, a very capable individual was identified to take my place.

I was appointed CEO of MEDIC in October 2006, and I was at peace with my decision. I felt it was an answer to my prayer. Just after leaving Baptist, the potential sale fell through, and the board entered into a management contract with a third party. Several of my colleagues lost their jobs, and I would likely have also if I had stayed. (Note: fast-forward another year—the Baptist Health System announced a merger with a crosstown health system.)

The timing of my resignation from Baptist may not have been ideal, but I am convinced it was the right decision. Much like previous job transitions in my career, I felt a sense of peace. I was excited to embark on a new challenge and knew it was right for me and my family. I saw it as an opportunity to use my education and experience in a different setting. Ironically, it would be the only time in my career that almost every aspect of my education and experience would be needed.

COMPASSIONATE LEADERSHIP

I felt peace for the first time in years when I accepted the new job. I could finally be the kind of leader that I had worked to become for three decades. I could have time for myself and my family. Time to get to know my people. Time to care. There is no need to prove my management stamina with brutal hours and cold, hard stares that should have been left behind in the ice age ... Is this heaven?

CHAPTER 13

A NEW DAY DAWNING

> *The entire healthcare field was challenged to adapt to a new paradigm. Unfortunately, the stable environment I had looked forward to when I left the hospital world didn't look nearly so stable after all.*

MEDIC Regional Blood Center is the primary supplier of blood and blood products for hospitals in a twenty-five-county service area in East Tennessee and southern Kentucky. Its main location is in Knoxville, and three additional satellite donor centers have opened in recent years.

MEDIC is a not-for-profit, independent, community blood center with a board of directors composed of physicians and community leaders. Founded in 1958 through a joint effort of the Knoxville Academy of Medicine and local hospitals, its mission is to provide a safe, adequate, and economical supply of blood and blood-related products and services.

The transition to MEDIC was similar to other job transitions I had experienced. I spent a significant amount of time meeting people, learning what they did, and understanding their roles. I also listened a lot and developed relationships.

True to form, the *25-50-25* rule also came into play. About 25 percent of the staff welcomed change, while another 25 percent resisted. In addition, I also had to adjust to an entirely new business model, and the learning curve was steep. While my hospital background was beneficial, I had to develop a different mindset, which took time. It didn't just happen overnight.

The opportunity at MEDIC also proved to have a few other refreshing benefits that I did not fully anticipate. I brushed up on hematology (the study of blood), a subject I had studied years earlier while working on my microbiology degrees. I also leveraged the knowledge and experience I had gained through my healthcare administration education and career. I could put myself in the shoes of our hospital customers.

The broader knowledge of the business world I had obtained through the MBA program also proved to be valuable. For the first time in my career, I used every aspect of my formal education and professional experience, all under one roof.

Another major benefit to making the move came in the form of time and a more balanced lifestyle. The life of a hospital CEO is demanding. Early-morning and late-night meetings are the norm, as are six-, sometimes seven-day workweeks.

After just a few months of working at MEDIC, I developed a new appreciation for the world outside hospitals. I could devote the time necessary to do my job and still have a life outside of work. I enjoyed family time and other leisure activities during the week, which never happened while working in the hospital. The other bonus was the time I gained on weekends to pursue new hobbies and recreational interests. More importantly, I was able to spend more time with my wife as she continued her rehabilitation.

DÉJÀ VU ALL OVER AGAIN

MEDIC is much smaller than any of the hospitals where I had worked, and the organizational structure is not nearly as complex. In some ways, the environment is like that of hospitals. The education and training of the staff are much the same as in a hospital, but the relative proportions of specialized staff and how their training is applied are very different. In a hospital, nurses, technicians, and therapists render patient care.

Blood centers, however, don't have patients and don't provide patient care. Rather, they have volunteer donors who willingly devote time to donating blood. In addition to nurses and technicians, blood centers rely heavily on phlebotomists, specially trained in venipuncture and blood collection.

To the public, a blood center looks much like a clinic or any other healthcare facility. Donors interact with receptionists, nurses, and phlebotomists, and defined protocols are followed. As part of the donor screening process, there is a brief physical examination consisting of blood pressure, pulse, temperature, and a finger stick to determine hemoglobin levels. Aseptic precautions such as alcohol preps, gloving, and other procedures are closely adhered to, much like a patient might experience in a physician's office. After being screened, the donor moves to a donor bed (i.e., recliner), where the actual donation procedure occurs. To the donor, the process is very similar to that of a clinic.

One of my biggest challenges was to train myself to use the term "donor" rather than "patient." After working thirty years in hospitals, that was not an easy habit to break, but it was all part of that steep learning curve. Behind the scenes, blood center operations are more akin to a manufacturing environment. Without getting into too much detail, blood centers follow several essential steps of a very elaborate process, leading to the "manufacturing" of a unit of transfusable blood or blood product.

Donor recruitment, blood collection, testing, component manufacturing, labeling, and distribution are all critical steps in the process. Furthermore, since the Food and Drug Administration highly regulates blood centers, every aspect of how a unit of blood is processed must adhere to strict standard operating procedures.

In addition to a long list of differences between blood centers and hospitals, I had to adjust to two other obvious differences. The first was the revenue model of a blood center. In a hospital, I was accustomed to multiple reimbursement methodologies, many of which required submitting a bill to a third party, waiting for approval or denial of an insurance claim, and then sending a balance bill to the patient. That was a very time-consuming and agonizing process that all hospitals had to deal with just to be compensated.

In a blood center, the revenue is essentially a function of product pricing and the volume of products distributed to hospitals. Thus, the billing and collection process is relatively simple in comparison. The blood center sends a monthly bill to the hospital for the blood and blood products used during the month. In turn, the hospital sends payment back to the blood center. There are no third parties, insurance companies, or patients to deal with. It was a welcome change.

A second major difference was that the blood center had no medical staff. Most blood centers the size of MEDIC have one physician, either as an employee or contractor, who serves as medical director. This differs greatly from a hospital medical staff, which could number several hundred physicians. As a hospital CEO, I was accustomed to dealing extensively with physician-related issues. Interacting daily with just one physician was a significant change.

ANOTHER DIFFICULT TRANSITION

There are pros and cons to working in a small organization. The good is that it doesn't take long to learn your way around and get to know people. Everyone at MEDIC was very welcoming and eager to help, and I felt at home almost immediately. Our administrative offices were accessible, and employees were routinely in and out of our offices.

However, a small organization's culture can be somewhat imposing. The physician who is credited with founding MEDIC in 1958 was a beloved figure. Anyone who worked for or with him has nothing but glowing things to say about him. Because of his influence, MEDIC had a culture much like a family-owned business.

Everyone knew everyone, and it was a family atmosphere. But there were also times when that family atmosphere meant that people got too much into other people's business, which posed problems. The rumor mill was alive and well, like none other I had experienced. I was amazed at how quickly a rumor could take on a life of its own.

Consequently, my honeymoon period was relatively short lived. The 25 percent who didn't want anything to change dug in their heels. I felt like I was running into a brick wall each time I suggested something be done differently. I found the organizational culture to be extremely rigid. I also found it challenging to live up to the standards set years before by MEDIC's founder. He left such a strong legacy, and I was reminded almost daily of how he would have handled certain situations.

Then, similarly, although to a lesser extent, I also had to work in the shadows of my immediate predecessor and friend who had just retired. He had served as CEO of MEDIC for twenty years and had been handpicked by MEDIC's founder. As part of his agreed-upon retirement transition, he continued in a limited role with MEDIC for several months after his official retirement. As such, he came into the office one day per week to work on special projects requested by the board.

Although he no longer had official management authority, his mere presence in the building was sometimes awkward. I want to be clear that he in no way interfered with my job and he didn't get involved with day-to-day issues. He was very respectful of me, which I appreciated.

There were times, however, when employees would see him and bend his ear about their concerns. That posed problems at times, but to his credit, he always deferred to me as the one with authority. In retrospect, it worked as well as expected and was only for a limited time. However, it did create confusion among employees who were unclear about his role.

Perhaps the more significant challenge was that I had a much different management style and saw things differently than he did. I found myself hesitant to make changes that I felt needed to be made. Sometimes, I would overthink decisions because I needed time to process and anticipate how he might react.

As a friend and valued colleague, the last thing I wanted to do was create unnecessary tension. Therefore, I was deliberate with my decision-making and made changes only when convinced they were needed. I know I made decisions and implemented changes he disagreed with, but he never second-guessed me. I am proud to say that we remain good friends to this day, and I appreciate his professionalism as we navigated through a somewhat awkward transition.

ADJUSTING TO A NEW CULTURE

The relatively small size of the organization posed some unique challenges relative to the management structure. With approximately 135 employees, the size of and expertise required by the management team were somewhat challenging to determine. Because of the regulated environment and the unique complexities of the blood industry, specific skills were needed in addition to the typical skills and expertise required by other organizations.

I was also mindful that we didn't need a management team as large as those I was accustomed to in the hospital environment. Finding that delicate balance was challenging. I also inherited a management team that was used to a certain style and structure. Making changes would not be easy. With time, however, I identified areas that I felt needed to be tweaked, as well as other opportunities for improvement.

I'm not sure if it was the size of the organization or the organizational culture, but I found making changes to the organizational structure to be especially challenging. The management team's personality changed whenever someone left and a new person joined the team. I learned a lot about interpersonal dynamics but can't say I found the right formula.

I respected each person's skills and expertise, along with the collective competence of our management team. But molding them into a high-performing team was difficult. I learned that high levels of competence, expertise, and a few strong personalities generated diverse perspectives. Balancing those diverse perspectives and getting everyone willing to see the other person's point of view was difficult to achieve.

I have always prided myself on being a team player. I learned the value of teamwork at a very young age while playing team sports. Each position is different, but all contribute to the team's success. Once I moved into leadership positions, I saw myself taking on the role of a coach. I may not have had the unique skills to play each position, but I recognized the need for everyone to work together.

One coach that I always admired was John Wooden, the legendary basketball coach at UCLA. Who could argue with his coaching accomplishments—an 80 percent winning record, ten national championships, and an eighty-eight-game winning streak?[39]

In his book *Wooden on Leadership*, he emphasizes the importance of teamwork, using the analogy that "it takes ten hands to score a basket."[40] One player may ultimately put the ball through the hoop, but every player on the floor contributes.

Teamwork is simple in theory but sometimes difficult to achieve. I found myself struggling to mold a high-performing team ... not because of each team member's expertise but because of their varied perspectives.

A professional colleague recommended that I read *The Five Dysfunctions of a Team* by Patrick Lencioni.[41] This book was an excellent synopsis of understanding what makes teams work effectively and analyzing the problems that keep talented teams from reaching their potential. It is a book that I would highly recommend to any aspiring leader.

---

39   Mike Puma, "Wizard of Westwood," ESPN Classic, accessed November 19, 2024, https://www.espn.com/classic/biography/s/Wooden_John.html.

40   John Wooden, *Wooden on Leadership* (McGraw Hill, 2005).

41   Patrick Lencioni, *The Five Dysfunctions of a Team* (Jossey-Bass, 2002).

LIFE IN A FISHBOWL

Then there was the fishbowl effect. I mentioned earlier that sometimes, in small organizations, people tend to be in other people's business. In my position, it was as if everyone was watching every move I made. The configuration of our offices was such that people could see me coming and going. They knew my routines: when I got to the office and when I left.

They knew if I walked down the hall to the men's room. Almost everyone in the organization knew I was gone if I was out of the building for an extended period. They may not have known where I went but knew I was gone. Some would even speculate where I was, and then the rumors started flying. Over time, I got used to it.

Similarly, there were times when people knew who I was meeting with behind closed doors. Again, because of our office configuration, it was apparent when my door was closed for any reason. As a routine practice, I held private meetings with my direct reports, mainly to conduct conversations of a sensitive or confidential nature. Those private conversations were intended for the parties involved, not to be shared with others.

The frustrating thing, however, was that there were times when other people tended to assume that specific topics were being discussed and decisions were being made. I was often criticized for supporting the point of view of certain people and thereby accused of playing favorites. Looking back, I am disappointed that people arrived at wrong conclusions based on limited information. They inappropriately interpreted some decisions as being biased without the benefit of knowing all the facts. But I suppose that is human nature.

Due to the nature of those closed-door, confidential conversations, however, I wasn't free to share information and explain why I made decisions I made. That is a delicate aspect of leadership that many people don't always understand. There will be times when only you have all the facts, but for confidential reasons, those facts can't be shared publicly.

NO LONGER A STABLE INDUSTRY

CRUCIBLE #8:

PATIENT BLOOD MANAGEMENT AND THE 2008 RECESSION

Patient blood management (PBM) was introduced in 2005 but didn't gain much traction until a few years later. Essentially, this concept changed the focus from the product (i.e., a unit of blood) to the patient. Hospitals and clinicians began scrutinizing blood transfusions from the standpoint of patient safety and cost, resulting in decreased blood utilization. About the same time that these new protocols were being adopted, the US experienced an economic recession. Together, these two developments placed significant pressure on the blood industry. [42]

The blood industry is unique because it serves a narrow but critical niche. One could argue that the availability of safe transfusable blood is one of the most vital pieces of the larger healthcare puzzle, yet it is downstream of what is happening in the hospital. Blood and blood products are generally administered to patients in a clinical setting, primarily hospitals, under the order and direction of a physician.

---

42   R. R. Gammon, N. Almozain, A. Jindal, et al., "Patient Blood Management, Past, Present and Future," *Annals of Blood* (September 2024), accessed October 25, 2024.

As such, the demand for blood depends on physicians' clinical decisions. Unlike the products of other related industries (i.e., pharmaceuticals, medical devices, etc.), blood centers can't create a demand for blood through marketing and advertising. And since a unit of blood has a limited forty-two-day shelf life, blood can't be stored indefinitely. While blood centers are expected to collect enough blood to serve their hospitals' needs, they must also be mindful of how much blood they need to collect.

For many years, blood centers' strategy was to collect as much blood as possible. It would either be distributed to hospitals or discarded when outdated. Shortly after I joined MEDIC, the paradigm changed. Hospitals placed more emphasis on Patient Blood Management (PBM), a focused effort to decrease blood utilization. Two primary factors drove this.

First, publications in the medical literature questioned the amount of blood being transfused in US hospitals. Clinical studies have shown that many disease processes can be managed just as well by transfusing less blood. Many studies also concluded that transfusing more blood than needed was putting patients at higher risk for other complications. In comparison to other countries around the world, the utilization of blood in US hospitals was on the high end. Consequently, hospitals began to take notice and implement PBM programs.

A second driving force was the cost of blood transfusions. In today's world, where there is a heightened awareness of rising healthcare costs, hospitals have begun scrutinizing every line item in their expense budget to find opportunities to reduce costs. PBM allowed hospitals to reduce the cost of blood and blood-product procurement, thereby reducing that budgeted expense.

It should be noted, however, that there were many counterarguments related to that strategy. The most notable was the relatively small portion of the total cost of transfusion attributed to the blood product itself. Other costs, such as labor, product storage, and the logistics of administering a blood transfusion, should not be overlooked.

The spotlight on PBM had a significant and measurable effect on blood centers nationwide. As more and more hospitals placed additional focus on reducing blood utilization, blood centers were forced to revisit their blood collection strategy. No longer could they collect as much blood as possible.

If too much blood was collected, significant units of blood would be outdated and, therefore, discarded. Since the blood center had already incurred the cost to collect and process the blood, it could not recoup those costs if the blood was not distributed to a hospital. The volume component of the revenue equation of price times volume was dramatically affected, and the profitability of blood centers was compromised.

The number of units of blood that a blood center needed to collect each day varied based on current inventory and projected utilization. An even more challenging issue was that the number of units of each blood type (A, B, O, AB) to be collected became increasingly important. Collecting the "right type" at the "right time" became the new strategy.

The number of units projected to be collected also impacted the number of blood drives and the number of donor appointments. Everything from supplies to resource allocation and staffing levels was affected.

Competition between blood centers heated up as a result. As blood utilization declined, leading to a decline in revenues, blood centers looked for new geographical territories to expand into. The thinking behind this strategy was to make up for the declining volume by adding new hospital customers.

This resulted in a competitive environment among neighboring blood centers that had not existed previously. It also led to competitive bidding for hospital contracts, and consequently, the blood center's product pricing strategy became even more critical.

Historically, it was common practice for blood centers to make routine product pricing adjustments to cover increased operational costs. These adjustments were passed on to the hospitals as price increased.

Suddenly, however, pricing adjustments had to be carefully analyzed from a competitive standpoint, especially if multiple blood centers were bidding on the same hospital contract. Many blood centers held off making price adjustments, and some even lowered their prices to be more competitive. The blood center revenue model of price times volume just took another major hit. Both key components of the equation had been affected.

Then, in 2008, blood centers also had to adjust to one of the most devastating US economic recessions in several decades. Businesses that historically hosted company-sponsored blood drives were significantly impacted. Many companies reduced their workforce, while others were forced to close their doors.

As a result, the pool of potential blood donors began to shrink, and mobile-blood-drive scheduling got more complicated. Blood centers resorted to strategically placing bloodmobiles in public spaces such as retail parking lots, hoping (and praying) that donors would respond.

The entire healthcare field was challenged to adapt to a new paradigm. Unfortunately, the stable environment I had looked forward to when I left the hospital world didn't look nearly so stable after all.

A FRIGHTENING ENCOUNTER

CRUCIBLE #9:

ROBBED AT GUNPOINT

Just a few years after my wife's accident, I also experienced one of those "life happens" crucibles. One evening, as I was leaving work, I was robbed at gunpoint in the MEDIC employee parking lot. It was another life-changing event that still resonates today.

I had been at MEDIC for about five years when another one of those "life happens" crucibles raised its ugly head. It was November 2011, and I was leaving for home one evening after a long day at work. It was about 6:30 in the evening, and it was already dark.

As usual, I walked out of our building, crossed the street to our employee parking lot, and got into my car. While buckling my safety belt, I heard a tap on my window. I lowered the window, thinking it was one of our employees who wanted to talk or ask me a question.

However, I saw a stranger dressed in a hooded sweatshirt, holding an unlit cigarette in his fingers.

He lifted the cigarette to his lips and said, "Hey, buddy, do you have a light?"

I told him, "No, I don't smoke," and started rolling my window back up.

Then, in the blink of an eye, I saw a handgun pointed at my head about three inches from my left temple. He then said, "Give me your wallet."

My nerves at that point were shot, and I began shaking as I tried to unbuckle my safety belt. I guess I was taking too much time, so he said, "Don't make me do it. Don't make me do it."

I responded, "I am going to give you my wallet; just give me time."

It was all I could do to get my safety belt unbuckled and get to my wallet. Once I retrieved my wallet from my back pocket, I handed it to him, and he was off in a flash. He jumped into a getaway car and was gone within seconds.

Stunned and incoherent, I exited my car and started walking back to my office. All I could think of at that time was to get to a phone and call the police. Within a few steps, I ran into one of our employees who was leaving the building, and she sensed that I was visibly upset. When I told her what had happened, she immediately pulled out her cell phone and called 911.

It didn't dawn on me that I could have done the same thing. My cell phone was on a clip on my belt, and all I needed to do was use it. But my mind was so clouded and confused that I wasn't thinking clearly. Thankfully, she was the voice of reason and helped me stay calm. Within a few minutes, the police arrived, but the culprits were long gone.

I have reflected on that incident many times over the years. Much like my wife's accident, it had a long-lasting impact on how I view life. That employee may not have been my guardian angel who saved my life, but she was there to help just the same.

I shudder to think what could have happened. The robber could have pulled the trigger. He could have stolen my car. He could have carjacked me and taken me to a remote location where he could have shot or harmed me. But through God's grace, I am still alive and well.

My wallet only had a few dollars of cash in it, but gone were my driver's license, credit cards, family photos, and a few other personal items. The culprits made a few purchases using my credit cards within minutes of the robbery. I never recovered my wallet or any of its contents; it took months to sort that out.

Yes, I would consider that a life-altering experience. I developed a whole new perspective on the value of life. I fully understand that the story could have ended much differently. It was yet another reminder of how important it is to appreciate the people in your life, whether they be family, friends, or coworkers.

I know for a fact this incident had a tremendous influence on how I view the world around me. I hope it served as a positive reinforcement that my job and the opportunity to work for an organization like MEDIC should be seen as a privilege, not to be taken for granted.

COMPASSIONATE LEADERSHIP

There is nothing—*nothing*—that compares with having a gun in your face to get your personal priorities in order. Life is not all about working. You never know when it can be snatched away. Leave nothing undone. Leave nothing unsaid. Hug your kids. Walk in the rain. Enjoy a sunrise.

CHAPTER 14

YOU GOTTA HAVE HEART

> *People who work in healthcare will frequently use the words "heart for service" and "compassion for our fellow man" to describe their calling. It is central to their very being.*

Several years ago, while living in Middle Tennessee, my wife and I had season tickets to the Broadway series at the Tennessee Performing Arts Center in Nashville. One of the more memorable performances was *Damn Yankees* with the lead role played by the great Jerry Lewis.

In one scene of the play, the manager of the Washington Senators baseball team tries to instill enthusiasm, encouragement, and confidence in his team as they prepare to face the hated New York Yankees. The song "Heart" became an iconic musical score of that Broadway production.

Throughout history, the word "heart" has been used to illustrate different things. As a reference to one of the human body's most vital organs, "heart" is typically used when describing a central theme.

It has been used to describe emotions, feelings, and generosity.

It has been used to describe love, passion, and commitment.

In the case of the Washington Senators in the play *Damn Yankees*, it referred to courage. But it can also be used as a synonym for compassion, and that hits home with me.

> *People who work in healthcare will frequently use the words "heart for service" and "compassion for our fellow man" to describe their calling. It is central to their very being.*

My tenure as CEO of MEDIC lasted sixteen and a half years. It was the longest tenure at any one organization during my entire career, and I consider it an honor to have worked with such a great team for those many years. In many ways, my time at MEDIC served as a personally gratifying capstone to my professional career. It allowed me to make a meaningful contribution and be of service to the community.

That is not to say that it was without challenges. The blood industry continued to change at a fast pace, as did anything and everything associated with healthcare. There were ups and downs, highs and lows, successes and failures. However, once I adjusted to the smaller organization and understood its unique culture, I was able to enjoy a bit of personal and professional satisfaction.

Irrespective of the challenges that are inherent to leaders of any organization, I feel good about what was accomplished during those years. Most of all, I found MEDIC's mission, and the valuable service it provides to the community, to align with my values. That was enough to keep me focused and motivated.

ANOTHER IMPORTANT MILESTONE

I mentioned earlier that the transition from the hospital to MEDIC provided relief from the relentless demands on my time. For the first time since the early years of my career, I could enjoy a more balanced lifestyle. But the extra personal time also came with a catch.

I am the type of person who likes to fill every minute of every day doing something productive. With more free time on my hands, I started feeling the urge to scratch an itch that I had for many years, and that was to earn a terminal academic degree.

I was mindful that some people jokingly referred to me as a "professional student" since I had already earned an undergraduate and three master's degrees. However, I had to prove to myself that I could achieve more. The Medical University of South Carolina offered a three-year Doctor of Health Administration (DHA) program that suited me perfectly.

The program required two years of on-campus coursework consisting of quarterly, four-day class sessions in Charleston. Projects and writing assignments were then submitted online in between campus visits. The final year was devoted to research and writing a dissertation.

So much for having free time on my hands. The demands of the doctoral program, in addition to the demands of my full-time job, consumed almost all my time. I sacrificed family and leisure time to keep up with the pace. I found myself spending most nights and weekends writing papers and working on assignments that had deadlines. There was minimal downtime between quarters, so the cycle continued almost nonstop for two years.

The final dissertation year required even more self-discipline. There were no deadlines other than certain milestones mutually agreed upon between my faculty advisor and me. The burden was on me to conduct the research, write the manuscript, and prepare my defense.

I had heard that some doctoral students never earned their degrees because they didn't have the discipline to finish the dissertation requirement.[43] I was determined not to be one of those students. As a result, I completed all requirements, including my dissertation defense, ahead of schedule.

I have often been asked if it was worth it. From a career standpoint, probably not. It neither earned me a promotion nor a pay raise. As a side benefit, however, it did lead to some part-time teaching opportunities at local academic institutions. I had no interest in teaching full time, but I was open to part-time opportunities. Teaching a few courses also served as an incentive for me to keep learning and challenged me to stay up to date on current issues.

Mostly, however, earning a doctorate gave me a huge sense of personal accomplishment, and that is a very gratifying feeling. Only about 2 percent of the US population holds a doctoral degree. I feel honored and proud to be among that 2 percent.[44]

THE MOTHER OF ALL CRUCIBLES

CRUCIBLE #10:

COVID-19

On March 11, 2020, the WHO declared the novel coronavirus (COVID-19) outbreak a global pandemic. WHO Director-General Dr. Tedros Adhanom Ghebreyesus noted that over the past two weeks, the number of cases outside China had increased thirteenfold and the number of countries

---

43   "67 Doctorate Degree Statistics and Facts," National University, accessed December 4, 2024, https://www.nu.edu/blog/doctorate-degree-statistics/#:~:text=About%20 2%25%20of%20the%20U.S.%20Population%20Holds%20a%20PhD.

44   "PhD Percentage by Country / Number of Doctorate Degrees per Country 2024," World Population Review, accessed December 4, 2024, https://worldpopulationreview.com/country-rankings/phd-percentage-by-country.

with cases had increased threefold. Further increases were expected.

He said that the WHO was "deeply concerned both by the alarming levels of spread and severity and by the alarming levels of inaction," and he called on countries to take action now to contain the virus. [45]

I suppose it is human nature to dismiss developments in other countries as being too remote to impact those of us close to home. Such was the case in late 2019 and early 2020. Here in the US, we began to hear reports of a virus in China that produced serious flu-like symptoms, and in some cases, death for people exposed to it.

We began hearing the term "coronavirus" mentioned in the national media, but like many other reports, many of us didn't take it very seriously. After all, how could something halfway across the globe affect us here? Surely it would run its course and quickly become an obscure event.

However, by the spring of 2020, the spread of coronavirus, or COVID-19 as it was more accurately referred to by then, became more real. We heard daily reports of a pending outbreak and were encouraged to take precautions. National, regional, and local public health officials warned us to take it seriously, and true to form, the national media couldn't let a good crisis pass without fueling the flames of panic. In mid-March, the WHO declared a worldwide pandemic, and our whole life changed.

---

45   D. Cucinotta and M. Vanelli, "WHO Declares COVID-19 a Pandemic," *Acta Biomed* (March 19, 2020), accessed October 25, 2024, https://pubmed.ncbi.nlm.nih. gov/32191675./.

I attended the annual meeting of America's Blood Centers, our national blood association, in Washington, DC, in early March 2020. After the meeting, following two days of updates on other important issues, a town hall session was scheduled to discuss the topic of COVID-19.

By then there had been a lot of information (and misinformation) in the media, and it was deemed an important enough issue to merit attention. So much about the spread of the virus was unknown, but we knew that blood centers and our daily lives would potentially be affected.

I have reflected on that town hall discussion many times, and in retrospect, I consider it to have laid the groundwork for what was to come. But, even then, I'm not sure we fully appreciated the real impact it would have. The meeting concluded on March 4, 2020.

I flew home the next day on a plane with very few people wearing masks. Wearing a mask never even crossed my mind. One week later, on March 11, the WHO issued its pandemic declaration. That day gave birth to the mother of all crucibles.

The last thing I wanted to deal with at that point in my career was a pandemic. By then, I had forty-five years of professional experience under my belt, and I was starting to think about retirement. I had fought enough battles and was ready to kick back and enjoy the rest of my life. But that was not in the cards. In fact, it was just the opposite. I had to kick into another gear and prepare for a rough, intense road ahead.

As the pandemic evolved, so did our daily routines. Each day brought new challenges, many exacerbated by new information (and misinformation) reported in the news media. As an organization, we were blazing new territory. Every day was a learning experience, and blood centers were forced to implement new processes, procedures, and protocols.

Within a few days of the WHO proclamation, we were barraged by questions from our staff and the public. Everyone was understandably concerned about their health and the health of their families. We initiated senior management meetings every morning to discuss the latest developments and information reported by the press. We tried, as best we could, to provide ongoing updates to our staff and our hospital customers. That proved challenging because of the widely diverse information reported by various news outlets.

Initially, we were optimistic that the pandemic might not be as widespread as originally reported. During those first few days, there were very few cases reported in Tennessee; then, slowly but surely, more cases were reported, and the first case in Knox County was confirmed. Our initial feeling of optimism suddenly faded, and reality set in.

Over several days, we were forced to cancel blood drives. A key concern was the tight confines of a bloodmobile where people were just a few feet from each other. Social distancing was virtually impossible. It became apparent that the mission of our organization was in jeopardy. If blood drives were canceled and donors didn't feel comfortable donating, where would we get the blood necessary to serve our hospitals?

In a matter of weeks, virtually all mobile blood drives were canceled. Thankfully, many of our loyal donors still wanted to help and, ironically, the news media provided some assistance. When asked in a nationally televised interview what the general population could do to help, the US Surgeon General advised people to donate blood if they were eligible. It didn't take long for our fixed donor sites to see an increase in donors.

While we appreciated the outpouring of support, the influx of donors also posed some significant logistic issues. Our waiting rooms became overcrowded, so we had to quickly implement new social distancing protocols.

We removed some of our waiting room furniture to control the number of people in confined spaces. We implemented daily temperature checks for our staff, donors, and visitors and encouraged donors to self-defer from donating if they weren't feeling well. Hand sanitizers were strategically located, and six-foot social distancing floor markers were placed throughout the building. Masks were recommended during those first few weeks, then later mandated as other businesses began doing so. We also implemented an appointment-only donor policy as a means of traffic control.

At about the same time, there was a decrease in blood utilization when hospitals began curtailing elective surgeries. In retrospect, that gave us some breathing room to adjust our collection procedures and implement new strategies. It was far from business as usual, and as the pandemic evolved, we used the opportunity to be creative. We learned that adversity often fuels creativity, and our staff should be commended for their ingenuity.

We benefited from another significant development when COVID-19 convalescent plasma (CCP) rose to the forefront. Essentially, people infected with COVID-19 had built up antibodies in their bloodstream as a normal immune mechanism to fight the disease. Those antibodies could potentially be used to treat other people by transfusing plasma from individuals who had recovered from COVID-19 to patients who were battling the disease.

Because of the specialized instrumentation and staff expertise, blood centers were seen as the logical collection site for CCP. Through the collective efforts of several organizations, an agreement was structured with federal agencies for blood centers to collect CCP and be reimbursed by the government.

Within a matter of weeks, our staff was trained, equipment was programmed for use, new supplies were ordered, and we started collecting CCP. It was one of those moments that made us proud to serve our fellow man in a very meaningful way.

Much has been written about the overall impact of the COVID-19 pandemic, and that is well beyond the scope of this book. Suffice it to say that it impacted every aspect of our personal and professional lives.

It was a major disruption like we had not seen before, and we are still dealing with the aftermath. We were severely impacted by supply chain issues and delivery delays of critical supplies. We learned that "just in time" delivery wasn't always just in time.

We dealt with the mask/no-mask debate, the vaccination/no-vaccination debate, and the transition to virtual meetings. We also dealt with short tempers, unhappy donors, and low staff morale. But through it all, we persevered.

Once the spread of the disease started to wane and things slowly returned to some semblance of normal, we faced the challenge of ramping back up our collections. As hospitals resumed scheduling elective surgeries, we had to quickly resume a full schedule of blood drives to keep pace with the demand for blood. Staffing challenges surfaced as a critical issue once people started returning to work.

The healthcare field was especially impacted as many healthcare professionals suffered from burnout due to the added workloads during the height of the pandemic. Many healthcare workers chose early retirement or left the field entirely, which added to staffing pressures. Competition for trained talent forced hospitals and other healthcare-related organizations to adjust pay scales to recruit and retain staff. Economic inflation also added to the pressures.

Reflecting on those tumultuous months, I now see that much was learned out of necessity. We learned to adopt new ways of doing things and the importance of *thinking out of the box*. We learned to be nimble and act quickly, more like a speedboat than a battleship. We learned the importance of timely communication among our staff and customers, even if the messaging was different from one day to the next.

From a leadership perspective, I learned the importance of remaining calm and not letting my emotions get the best of me. It was important to provide consistent and objective leadership, even in the face of chaos. It was important to make decisions based on the most credible information available at the time.

Most of all, it was important to focus on the most pressing issues. In some ways, I found myself developing a personal hierarchy of needs and jumping from one level to another multiple times during the day. There were organizational needs to be addressed. The mission of MEDIC was critical, and I, as CEO, was expected to see that the mission was fulfilled.

As an employer, it was important to be aware of the needs of our employees and their families. They were dealing with added pressures in their personal lives, and I needed to be sensitive to those pressures. From a personal standpoint, I had responsibilities as a husband and father. I knew that my family needed my support, and I needed to be mindful of the pressures they were dealing with. Finally, as self-serving as it may sound, I needed to remain mindful of my personal health and well-being.

Throughout the pandemic, I remained extremely cautious in my interactions with other people and followed all suggested protocols to avoid contracting COVID-19. Fortunately, I stayed healthy, and I am proud to say that I didn't miss a single day of work. As much as anything, I needed to set an example. If our employees were expected to come to work to maintain daily operations, I needed to do the same.

I can't let the topic of COVID-19 pass without giving a huge shout-out to my hospital colleagues. Even though I wasn't working in a hospital during that time, I remained close enough to know that they were going through some very difficult times. The influx of critically ill patients and the added burden it placed on healthcare workers is hard for me to comprehend. I am sure it was a nightmare.

If I haven't already done so, I want to acknowledge their leadership and express my appreciation for a job well done. In my opinion, not only did they answer the bell, but they did so in stellar fashion.

HANGING UP MY CLEATS

I have always been a huge sports fan. It didn't matter if it was football, basketball, baseball, or tiddlywinks. Like most kids who grew up in the 1960s, I had my favorite players. In baseball, my favorite players were Mickey Mantle, Roger Maris, and Willie Mays.

Years later, in the summer of 1972, I took a road trip to Houston with a college buddy to see the Astros play the New York Mets. As it turned out, we also had the good fortune of seeing Willie Mays play center field for the Mets, and a relative newcomer named Tom Seaver start as the Mets' pitcher.

Having begun his baseball career with the New York Giants in 1951 and moved with them to San Francisco in 1958, Willie Mays returned to New York to play for the Mets toward the end of his professional career. By then, he wasn't an everyday player, but he was still the great Willie Mays.

THE SAY HEY KID

As excited as I was to see the Say Hey Kid play, it didn't turn out as expected. On that day, Willie came to bat four times and struck out three. He also committed a critical fielding error by misjudging a routine fly ball.

It broke my heart to see one of baseball's all-time greats play so poorly, and unfortunately, that memory of Willie Mays will forever be etched in my mind. Like many athletes, he probably should have retired a few years earlier while still in his prime. His skills had diminished, and he no longer had the physical ability to compete with the younger players. Age has a way of doing that.

While I am not an elite athlete, the rigors of a nearly half-century healthcare career also eventually caught up with me. The decision to retire wasn't easy, but I am convinced it was the right decision at the right time. I didn't want to stay in the game so long that I started striking out and dropping routine fly balls.

In July 2022, I submitted my retirement notice to the MEDIC board of directors, to be effective April 30, 2023. I felt that the nine-month notice should provide sufficient time for the board to conduct a search for my replacement and allow me time to complete a few important items on my to-do list. I was also committed to working with the board to ensure an orderly transition in leadership.

I have always felt that it was essential to retire on my terms and not overstay my welcome. I knew that the day would eventually come when my skills would start to diminish and I would no longer be as effective as I once was.

After enduring two years of the intensity and prolonged aftermath of the COVID-19 pandemic, I sensed that my time had come. I can't say that I suffered from burnout, although the relentless challenge of navigating through the pandemic certainly took its toll. I didn't have much gas left in the tank, and I knew it was time to pass the torch to someone else.

There is also something to be said for new leadership. My healthcare career was overshadowed by rapid and significant change. However, the rate of change was beginning to accelerate even more with each passing year. Younger generations (i.e., millennials) see the world differently and in many ways push for change. I found it increasingly difficult to look at issues differently and recognized that the organization could benefit from a new set of eyes and a fresh approach.

In chapter 8, I shared observations from several of my most trusted professional colleagues. They didn't pull any punches and readily described the good, the bad, and the ugly. As I was collecting their input and stories, I concluded by asking each of them the same question, "If you had to do it all over again, would you still choose healthcare as a profession?"

I can honestly say, to a person, the answer was a resounding "yes." In so many words, they all referred to their healthcare career as a unique privilege. Some expressed reservations about the pressures of working in a hospital, yet they felt that a healthcare career required a special calling. To emphasize this notion, I share the following responses:

I would absolutely, positively state that I would do it all over again. This was the best career I could have ever imagined. While I think the environment has drastically changed, I would welcome the opportunity or the challenge to pursue the same opportunities again.

—Barton A. Hove, LFACHE

I absolutely would choose a healthcare career. Healthcare, for me, was a calling. It allowed me to fulfill a purpose on earth in which I could help people, show kindness, and be a small part of a dynamic industry.

—David N. Parmer, FACHE

I chose healthcare as a career while I was in high school. I worked in a Catholic hospital during the summer and was impressed by the "caring" work environment. When I began my professional career, my expectations were met ... service above self. There were challenges, but I have great memories and would definitely choose to work in healthcare again.

—Robert J. Humphrey, FACHE

Healthcare management is one of the most challenging careers anyone could choose because of the breadth of the personnel, from housekeepers to physicians, and the depth of the regulatory environment. However, influencing life-changing outcomes is so gratifying and rewarding that I would gladly spend my forty-plus years again as a healthcare executive.

—Jack Bryan

I think healthcare chose me rather than me choosing healthcare. The challenge, the excitement, and the unpredictability rank high on my list of reasons. The ladder for achievement has provided unlimited opportunities, and even after retiring, I continue to enjoy an active role in my community. Given the option to choose again, I would feel honored to be a part of the healthcare team.

—James D. Whitlock, DHA, LFACHE

WHEN LIFE AND DEATH ARE ON THE LINE

Throughout this book, I referenced several crucibles that significantly impacted my professional career and personal life. I am sure other people could recount events and developments just as significant. The following story, shared by a lifelong friend and colleague, illustrates the heart of leadership during an incredibly stressful time. It embodies important qualities such as courage, dedication, decisiveness, perseverance, and compassion. It also captures the overarching humanitarian spirit that uniquely characterizes healthcare workers.

With his permission, I share his story:

> I was the CEO of Tulane Medical Center in New Orleans in 2005. Because of its proximity to the Gulf of Mexico, New Orleans's geography lends itself to the possibility of hurricanes. Hurricane Katrina hit the area on Sunday night, August 29th, and the hospital lost power early Monday morning. Our initial action was to ensure that we had sufficient resources (i.e., food, water, medical supplies, personnel) to weather the storm. Then, we waited.
>
> On Monday, high winds and rain lasted throughout the day and eventually subsided around 6:00 p.m. Our survey of the property revealed minimal damage, which was encouraging. But the worst was yet to come.
>
> The levees of key waterways broke, and by midnight, we started to experience flooding and loss of electrical power. We had 150 inpatients, 15 were critical, and an additional 80 to 100 patients had been brought to the hospital by local authorities. There were also another 1,500 people through-

out our campus, including employees, family members, physicians, and students.

With the loss of power and the magnitude of the flood, it was apparent that a quick recovery would be unlikely, so we activated our evacuation plan. A local ambulance service was called around 3:00 a.m. on Tuesday, and they promised to provide helicopter support. The first helicopter arrived around noon, and we started by evacuating our most critical patients. Tulane's joint venture partner, HCA, also initiated a massive effort to secure additional helicopters to help with the evacuation effort.

We provided essential updates to employees and physicians throughout the day. There was limited phone service and no television reception, so we depended on satellite phones to keep us updated. Understandably, employees were very stressed, worrying about their families and homes.

By Wednesday evening, almost all patients, and some employees, had been evacuated. The Louisiana National Guard provided Chinook helicopters, which held about fifty people. On Thursday night, there were still about seven hundred people yet to be evacuated, including myself. Then by noon on Friday, everyone had been evacuated.

The next five and a half months were the most intense of my professional career. By mid-October, we received clearance to return to the hospital, and damage mitigation began. Ultimately, Tulane had to undergo significant reconstruction. The entire first floor needed to be gutted and rebuilt. Through it all, HCA remained very supportive that the hospital would reopen, which occurred in 2006, albeit with limited capacity.

The hurricane significantly damaged the entire city's healthcare infrastructure. Some area hospitals remained open, but others were forced to close. Of those that closed, a few reopened years later, while several remained closed permanently. Political battles over funding led to strained relationships between governmental officials and the private sector.

Tulane's employees and physicians were scattered across the country, and many never returned. Sadly, they chose to move their families and settle elsewhere. In the aftermath of Katrina, I had experiences that I had never had before. The emotional toll on employees and doctors was heavy. Several physicians came to me and broke down crying as they decided to move from New Orleans. This made a lasting impression on me.

As I reflect on that horrific experience, I am proud of our team's perseverance, and through the grace of God, no lives were lost. That is a blessing I have never forgotten.

—James T. Montgomery, FACHE

STRAIGHT FROM THE HEART

In my current hometown of Knoxville, Tennessee, the NBC affiliate television station, WBIR Channel 10, uses the phrase "Straight from the Heart" as its unique brand. It is intended to convey the station's genuine, heartfelt connection to the community and is used prominently in all newscasts and promotions. While the television field may be very different from healthcare, that simple message could be just as applicable.

COMPASSIONATE LEADERSHIP

In earlier chapters of this book, I expressed concern about where healthcare in the US is headed. We seem to have lost our sense of direction. Some feel that the entire healthcare delivery system is flawed and needs to be dismantled and rebuilt from the ground up. Attempts at "healthcare reform" have not solved all our problems.

Perhaps I am at that stage in life where I am starting to take more notice, but it seems like I am hearing more frequent complaints from friends and neighbors about how difficult it is to navigate the healthcare maze. Everything from understanding the health insurance quagmire and watching healthcare costs continue to rise to the impersonal feeling of just being a number and being shuffled through the system in assembly-line fashion.

I believe it is time for healthcare leaders to step up and revive the heart of leadership.

In the popular movie *The Wizard of Oz*, the Tin Man has a burning desire to have a heart. He is convinced that if he has a heart, he can feel the same emotions as human beings. He also wants to be able to love and care for others, qualities that he feels would make him a better person. To feed his desire, he willingly joins Dorothy in her quest to find the Wizard of Oz.

As much as I loved watching that movie during my younger years, I didn't easily identify with the Tin Man. As a human being, I could not envision what life would be like without a heart. It is at the very core of our existence as humans. As it turned out, the Tin Man already had a heart but didn't know how to use it.

How we use our hearts varies from person to person. Some have a heart for service; some have a heart for caring. Others have a heart for fame and fortune. Some are seen as being coldhearted. It is my hope that the healthcare field, and each individual working in healthcare, would exhibit the spirit of compassion that already resides in our collective hearts.

If it can happen for the Tin Man, surely it can happen for us.

EPILOGUE

> *I am only one, but still I am one. I cannot do everything, but still I can do something.*
>
> —*Edward Everett Hale*

As I put the final touches on the manuscript for this book, I have been retired for one year. As is my nature, however, I haven't sat still. I have continued to be involved with community organizations, volunteer opportunities, and church work. I consider that to be part of my personal mission. I also continue to teach college-level courses and have taken time to pursue new interests and hobbies.

Just as I was getting into a predictable retirement routine, another one of those pesky crucibles raised its ugly head ... I was diagnosed with prostate cancer. It wasn't unexpected since I have a family history of prostate cancer, and my PSA values have steadily increased over the past several years.

Once my PSA values reached a certain mark, my family physician referred me to a urologist for follow-up, and then a biopsy confirmed the diagnosis. After considering the various treatment options, I elected to undergo robotic surgery to remove the gland. My urologist was well trained in the latest surgery techniques, so I felt confident in my decision.

The tables had been turned. After all those years of working in hospitals, I suddenly found myself in the patient's shoes. I had to navigate through the complicated insurance maze and endure the hassles associated with the hospital admissions process. I now have a much better appreciation for healthcare consumers who must deal with all that red tape and remain calm and composed about their medical conditions. I learned to rely on my faith, my patience, and my family's support.

Aside from being concerned about my diagnosis and treatment, my hospital experience was a positive one. I was admitted to UTMC, and my surgery was the first case on a Thursday morning.

Everyone I encountered, from the admissions staff to the couriers, and the pre-op nurses, could not have been more courteous. The entire process was very efficient, and I felt that everyone went out of their way to ensure that my needs were met. Everything was explained in detail, and the staff answered all my questions. They made me feel like a person, not a number, and they did so with a high level of compassion.

Following surgery, as I woke up in the recovery room, I experienced more of the same. It was as if I were the only patient there. I felt that all eyes were on me. The staff was courteous and attentive. I was admitted overnight to one of the specialty units and couldn't help but be impressed with the level of technology and the sophistication of equipment in my hospital room. The fully automated bed, the computerized monitoring devices, and the electronic recordkeeping were all top-of-the-line.

As I lay in bed the next morning, waiting to be evaluated for discharge, I reflected on my first part-time job in that nursing home in the summer of 1968. I was amazed by all the medical advances made over those fifty-five years. Despite its flaws and shortcomings, I felt proud to be part of America's healthcare system.

Technology aside, what impressed me most was the personal touch of the hospital staff. The latest technology and the highest skill and clinical expertise would have been misdirected if deployed without the key ingredients of kindness and compassion. I am happy to say that my surgery was a success, and after a period of recovery, I am back to my routine activities of golf, pickleball, hiking, and jogging.

PERSONAL REFLECTION

Now, as I have come to the end of my professional career, I have taken time to reflect on what I accomplished and didn't accomplish. If I were so inclined, I could probably make a lengthy list of both. However, my list would likely differ significantly from what others might say about me. Family, friends, and professional colleagues view me from different perspectives. Consequently, their opinions of what I do well and not so well would certainly vary.

I think about the adversities I faced during my career ... those crucibles that seemed to alter my best-laid plans. Whether it be the difficult decisions I had to make, the rapidly changing healthcare environment, or the personal trauma I experienced, somehow, I was able to persevere.

That which did not kill me only made me stronger.

I also recognize that very little of what I accomplished or didn't accomplish really matters in the bigger picture. I think back on those experiences that prompted me to enter healthcare in the first place

… those hot summer days working on the farm in Louisiana, those elderly residents in the nursing home, and that young teenager with spinal meningitis who died during my shift as a respiratory therapist.

In retrospect, those experiences were probably mini crucibles that helped prepare me for more challenging times ahead. Those early experiences taught me meaningful lessons, the most important of which was compassion.

BAKER'S DOZEN OF LEADERSHIP TRAITS

I have been fortunate to know and learn from many seasoned healthcare executives during my career. I have had the opportunity to observe their unique styles and mannerisms, as well as their strengths and weaknesses. Based on those observations, I developed a baker's-dozen list of what I would consider to be the most important traits of a successful leader. Granted, my list is subjective, and not validated by empirical research. However, this list might be a simplified template for future healthcare leaders.

☐ **Industry Knowledge**
Healthcare leaders must have a well-rounded understanding of the industry. Healthcare is changing very rapidly, and it is incumbent on leaders to stay abreast of those changes.

☐ **Communication Skills**
Effective leaders must have good verbal *and* written communication skills. They should also possess empathic listening skills.

☐ **People Skills**

As an extension of good communication, it is also imperative for effective leaders to have good people skills. But it is a two-edged sword. Leaders should be *friendly*, but also *firm* when holding others accountable.

☐ **Vision**

Successful leaders should have both short-term and long-term vision and be able to anticipate the future.

☐ **Thick Skin**

Being a leader isn't for the faint of heart. Steve Jobs is credited with saying, "If you want to make everyone happy, don't be a leader. Sell ice cream."

☐ **Good Judgment**

I credit Ray Brown and his book *Judgment in Administration* for emphasizing the importance of this key trait.

☐ **Character**

Some people define character as "how one acts when no one else is looking." A leader's reputation is a function of their conduct, both in the public eye and behind closed doors.

☐ **Business Savvy**

The healthcare field is very complex. Successful leaders should be willing to take risks to move the organization forward. Competition, financial challenges, and a rapidly changing environment add to the complexity.

☐ **Charisma**

This trait is somewhat subjective. There are leaders whose mere presence in the room commands respect. I think of Ronald Reagan with that handsome, imposing, articulate persona. Some people have that "it" factor.

☐ **Analytic Skills**

As healthcare has become more complex, this trait has risen in importance. Given the current state of healthcare and the financial challenges ahead, this may be one of the most important leadership traits.

☐ **Decisiveness**

A key trait of a successful leader is decisiveness. Sometimes, decisions must be made without all pertinent information being available. It is important to make decisions based on facts, not assumptions. It often means relying on your judgment.

☐ **Emotional Intelligence**

One of the college courses I teach uses a textbook written by Carson Dye, a healthcare consultant. In his book *Leadership in Healthcare: Essential Values and Skills*, Mr. Dye describes the importance of emotional intelligence. It means keeping your cool under duress, particularly when interacting with others.[46]

☐ **Compassion**

While I list this trait last, it should be no surprise that I consider compassion a vitally important leadership trait.

---

46   Carson F. Dye, *Leadership in Healthcare* (Health Administration Press, 2017).

> Throughout this book, there have been multiple references to compassion and its importance, especially in today's healthcare environment. It is the missing ingredient that needs to be revived.

I did not write this book from the perspective of an expert. It was from the perspective of an ordinary guy who was fortunate to work in leadership roles. I have fallen woefully short of achieving many of the above-listed traits.

But leaders are not robots; they are humans just like you and me. We all make mistakes and wish we had handled certain situations differently. I fully acknowledge that I was a very imperfect leader, but it didn't stop me from striving to do better every day.

While I have failed more times than I like to admit, my goal has always been to treat others the way I would want to be treated. It is the Golden Rule and one of the basic tenets of my faith-based upbringing.

SEALED WITH HEART AND COMPASSION

Growing up in a small town in the 1960s, I enjoyed reading our local weekly newspaper, *The Plainsman-News*, to keep up with events around town. Like most other small-town newspapers, there were stories of interest, wedding announcements, and obituaries. I especially liked reading about my friends and neighbors and recapping the results of local sporting events.

At the very top of the front page of my hometown newspaper, above the banner and leading headline, the following quote was printed in small, italicized letters:

I am only one, but still I am one. I cannot do everything, but still I can do something and because I cannot do everything, I will not refuse to do the something that I can do.

—Edward Everett Hale (1822–1909), author of "The Man Without a Country"

That quote is attributed to Edward Everett Hale, an American author, historian, and Unitarian minister in the late 1800s. I am no historian, and I know very little about Edward Everett Hale's life; however, as a young boy, that quote made an impression on me, and for some reason, it still resonates in my mind.

I want to think that my healthcare career reflects the meaning behind that quote. I know my limitations, and I recognize that I cannot do everything. But I sincerely hope that I did something, and I hope that I did so with a healthy dose of heart and compassion.

IN CLOSING

I have seen hundreds of healthcare executives come and go throughout my career. In previous chapters, I acknowledged several of my professional colleagues who embody the true spirit of servant leadership. Their knowledge, wisdom, and heart for service are evident. I would consider them to be role models for aspiring healthcare leaders.

On the other end of the spectrum, I have seen many young and very capable new executives enter the field. I can't help but be impressed with their intellect, their abilities, and their enthusiasm. I see qualities in them that I wish I had myself. I have been fortunate to get to know many of them, and from my perspective, healthcare is in good hands as we move into the future.

But there is a word of caution. With all the changes, with all the uncertainty, and with all the public outcry for better and more-affordable healthcare services, I would hope that the key element of *compassion* doesn't get lost in the shuffle.

Throughout my career, one of my favorite duties as CEO was welcoming new employees to the organization. It was an opportunity for me to meet each of them face to face, learn their names, and learn a little about them. Many were seasoned employees who had worked at other organizations. Some were just starting their careers. All were excited to begin a new journey.

I ended each orientation session with a few comments about consumer (i.e., patient, donor, etc.) expectations. I used some real-life examples of how we, as consumers, have predetermined expectations each time we purchase a good or service. Our expectations are either met, unmet, or exceeded based on our experience.

Then I added a final thought to the discussion. At the end of the day, consumers who seek healthcare services are expecting two things. First and foremost, they expect quality care. That is a given. If they did not expect to receive quality care at our organization, they would not even come through our door. They would seek care elsewhere.

Then, there is the second expectation. Consumers expect that the care is delivered in a kind and compassionate way. Therein lies the real lesson and the challenge for future leaders. Even with the most up-to-date training, all the technological developments, and the latest and greatest wonder drugs, healthcare is still a personal service rendered by people to people.

One could argue that the heart is the most vital organ in the human body. It is central to our very existence. I believe that it is also central to leadership. In the world of healthcare, where the health and well-being of others are at stake, I feel that the fundamental trait of a good leader is to possess a heart of leadership. It conveys values, character, and compassion. It conveys a desire to be of service to others and defines one's priorities. I would encourage future leaders to embrace these qualities and make them the primary motivation behind their career aspirations.

The importance of compassionate care must not be overlooked. It starts with a commitment to service. Whether it be patients, blood donors, employees, physicians, or professional colleagues, the heart of leadership must be preserved.

ABOUT THE AUTHOR

DR. JAMES L. (JIM) DECKER is a retired healthcare executive with over forty-seven years of distinguished leadership experience. He has held senior executive positions with four different hospitals and health systems in Tennessee and concluded his career as CEO of a regional blood center.

A native of Zachary, Louisiana, he holds BS and MS degrees in microbiology from Louisiana State University, a masters in science in hospital and health administration from the University of Alabama at Birmingham (UAB), a masters in business administration from the University of Tennessee, and a doctorate in health administration from the Medical University of South Carolina.

Honors include the UAB Graduate Program in Hospital and Health Administration Alumni Association Award for Academic Excellence (1977); Tennessee Hospital Association Meritorious Service Award for a Chief Executive Officer (1994); UAB Graduate Program in Hospital and Health Administration Alumnus of the Year (1995); Tennessee ACHE Regent's Award for Senior Level Healthcare Executive (2009); Outstanding Doctoral Student Award, Medical University of South Carolina (2013); Knoxville Business Journal Health Care Hero for Administrative Excellence (2017); Tennessee

Association of Blood Banks President's Award (2023); and MUSC College of Health Professions Distinguished Alumni Award (2023).

Dr. Decker is a Life Fellow in the American College of Healthcare Executives (ACHE) and past ACHE Regent for Tennessee. He is a former board member of the Tennessee Hospital Association, the Hospital Alliance of Tennessee, and America's Blood Centers, and has served on numerous boards of community organizations. He holds adjunct faculty appointments at South College and the University of Tennessee.

Among his honors and achievements, he is proudest to be a lifelong blood donor, having donated over forty-five gallons of blood during his lifetime. He resides with his wife, Michelle, in Knoxville, Tennessee, and has three grown children and three grandchildren.

www.ingramcontent.com/pod-product-compliance
Lightning Source LLC
Chambersburg PA
CBHW021924190326
41519CB00009B/895